Showing NATIVE PONIES

Showing NATIVE PONIES

JENNY MORGAN

Foreword By SIR HARRY LLEWELLYN

Kenilworth Press

First published in Great Britain 1994 by
The Kenilworth Press Limited
Addington
Buckingham MK18 2JR

British Library Cataloguing in Publication Data
A catalogue record for this book is available from the British Library

ISBN 1-872082-58-0

Illustrations by Debbie Dunbar
Plans by Katy Lane
Design by Paul Saunders
Typeset in Palatino 11/15
Typesetting and layout by The Kenilworth Press Ltd
Printed and bound in Great Britain by
WBC Book Manufacturers Ltd, Bridgend

Contents

Foreword

by Sir Harry Llewellyn, Bt, CBE

JENNY MORGAN'S treatise *Showing Native Ponies* is a valuable appraisal of the problems that are involved and advises experienced as well as inexperienced people as to how to proceed. She shows a real understanding of the problems and steps to be taken. She gives encouragement to owners who want to start taking an interest in ponies but who have had no previous knowledge or experience of them. I note that she advises people to handle the ponies as much as possible and this is a vital factor. To get the best results one must spend as much time as possible on our four-footed friends. I strongly recommend beginners as well as experienced pony owners to read this book and take the excellent advice offered.

*This book is dedicated to **Helen Forsyth***
– an example to us all

Acknowledgements

FIRSTLY, a big thank you to all the native ponies who have given us so much pleasure over the years – but especially to Chieveley Honey who started it all; to Aston Tinkerbell, who has given us so many great moments over the last sixteen years and is still going strong; to Coppice Drummer, who has enough character for several ponies; to Ballan Blodwen, our up-and-coming star; and most of all to Aston True Welshman – a very special pony indeed!

Thanks also to my daughter Emma, without whom there would have been no successful ridden ponies at all from this yard, and also to my daughter Julie, who 'holds the fort' when we are away at shows. Grateful appreciation is also due to my friend Julia Gibson, who drives the lorry, keeps me endlessly supplied with cups of tea and laughs, and held my hand during the birth of this book.

Thanks are also due to Sir Harry Llewellyn for his kind foreword; to Lesley Gowers of Kenilworth Press for her help and advice; and to all those breed society secretaries, and others too numerous to mention individually who supplied information and help so willingly; to Debbie Dunbar for her lovely drawings, and to Anthony Reynolds, John Birt, Chris Cook from Pleasure Prints and everyone else who kindly allowed us to use their photographs.

Finally, thanks to everyone who ever shared their body brush or hoof oil with me in the line-up, and to everyone who ever exhibited a pony for me when we were short staffed – they demonstrate the right spirit of showing. Long may you all continue to have fun!

Jenny Morgan
August, 1994

Photo credits
John Birt, cover, 41, 44 (both), 46, 49 (both), 50 (both), 60 (both), 62, 63; Chris Cook, Pleasure Prints, 39, 53, 54, 70, 77, 111, 119; Jenny Morgan, 18, 31; Anthony Reynolds, 17, 35, 45, 73, 86, 89, 93, 98, 101, 104, 112, 116, 118, 121.

Introduction

ALTHOUGH MOST of our native breeds are now clearly defined, in the history of the domestication of the horse the native stud books are very recent, most of them being less than a hundred years old. Many of our native breeds have the blood both of other 'cold blood' breeds and of eastern, or hot bloods. Some breeds have been crossed with one another in the past, such as the Fell and the Dales, and some have common ancestry, such as the Norfolk Roadster which appears in the history of both the Welsh Cob and the Dales. Arab ancestry is in fact common to many, including the Welsh and the New Forest. Even the best of our judges sometimes have difficulty in telling a Fell from a Dales, or a New Forest from a Welsh Section B!

What stars our native ponies are! They are ridden and driven, they take part in every conceivable event from showing to show jumping, and there is a native pony for every size, shape and ability of rider. They live and thrive outdoors in the worst of weather and on very little food, and usually with not much need of veterinary services. What more could you ask? Each of the breeds has its own, now clearly defined characteristics, but underlying these each has a strong heritage of hardiness, stamina, agility and adaptability.

The origin of our native ponies is lost in the mists of time. Shetland ponies were recorded as far back as 500BC, and the Exmoor pony is thought to date back even further, to prehistoric times. Most breeds were influenced by the introduction of three great oriental stallions: the *Darley Arabian*, the *Byerley Turk* and the *Godolphin Barb*. It is possible that these were crossed with the now extinct Galloway mares to produce ponies which were then crossed with other natives. Britain also once had another native breed, the Norfolk Trotter or Roadster. These served as foundation stock for other breeds, most noticeably the Welsh Cob.

In the 1800s the Norfolk Trotter was very similar to the present-day Welsh Cob, although larger and rather more influenced by oriental blood. His trotting prowess made him much in demand as a carriage horse, and indeed he is thought to be the forerunner of today's Hackney. The breed was directly descended from the aforementioned *Darley Arabian* via *Shales 699*, grandson of the Arab and sire of *Marshland Shales 435*. *Evolve*, descended from this bloodline, sired the famous *Mathrafal Brenin*, who through descendants such as *Brenin Gwalia* and *Mathrafal* have spread this blood throughout the Welsh Cob of today.

So next time you are riding your Welsh Cob and standing next in line to a Dales pony, remember that despite their distinctive differences today, less than two hundred years ago they probably shared a common ancestry, and they could well be related!

PART ONE

CHAPTER ONE

Choosing Your Pony

IF YOU have decided to buy a native pony, where do you start? First, you must decide which breed or breeds appeal to you. If you intend to ride the pony, it must be the right size for you or your children. If this is the first time you have purchased a pony, be sure that you have made all the necessary preparations such as living arrangements and also considered the 'running' costs. There are plenty of good books on these subjects.

WHICH BREED?

For whatever purpose you want your pony, there will probably be more than one breed to choose from. So the first thing to do might be to visit some shows. County and breed shows will give you a better selection of ponies to look at which are at the top end of their breed category.

Get a catalogue at the show and familiarise yourself with the names and the breeding of the ponies which appeal to you. Often you will find that the same prefixes come up again and again: these would be the studs to visit and the names to look out for in advertisements. You could also get a copy of the journal published by your chosen breed society; all of the societies publish an annual journal or suchlike. Look for studs which offer 'stock for sale' – some studs may have young, unbroken ponies, or broken but green ponies for sale.

All of the breed societies have a stand or caravan at county shows and other events where they give out leaflets and display pictures of their champions. Without exception, they are always pleased to give advice and information which may help you make a choice.

If you get to know exhibitors who show your chosen breed, then you will probably hear of a pony for sale from them. Most seasoned exhibitors know what is available for sale in their breed at any given time and can point you in the direction of a suitable purchase.

BUYING A PONY

Most ponies are bought through advertisements either in local papers or well-known national magazines such as *Horse and Hound*. Most ridden ponies are bought this way, since these are more likely to be found in private homes. If you are a novice purchaser, you will need to do a certain amount of research before you actually buy; you may well need to go and view several ponies before you make a decision. When you make your first enquiries, there are several questions which you should ask:

- If you are buying youngstock, ask for details of a pony's breeding; though remember, just because its full brother is a champion, it is no guarantee that this one will be successful. It is only a guide.

- Be sure that the breeder or present owner feels the pony will be suitable for your needs. If you intend to breed from a filly in the future, choose a good bloodline. If you intend to ride, go for a family that has proved itself reliable as ridden ponies.

- If you are buying a ridden pony, be sure that he is suitable for your ability and for the job that you want him to do. Just because he has won this and that with his present owners, it does not necessarily mean that he will be successful with you. They may well be far more experienced. And always

James and Gemma Entage with their Shetland friends, discussing the working hunter pony class. The right pony will give a child endless enjoyment.

remember, you cannot buy experience – or rosettes!

- If you want to start with novice ridden or brood mare classes you will need to ensure that your potential purchase is still a novice. The rules for novices vary from one society to another: get a copy of the rule book and check.

- It might be possible to get a video or photographs of ponies that might be suitable; and if you can see that they are not, this will save long wasted journeys.

- Always be quite sure that the pony has no vices such as wind-sucking or crib-biting, and that he is sound. The description 'free from vices' is a guarantee, in law, that the animal does not windsuck, crib-bite, box-walk or weave.

- Ask if the pony is registered and if it has breed society papers. It is quite possible for a pony to be described as, for example 'a Welsh pony' in an advertisement; but this does not mean that legally he has to be registered. And if he is not, he could not be shown in classes for registered ponies.

Buying from a breeder

If you want a young pony, often the best place to buy him is direct from his breeder. If the stud is well known, it is in their best interest to sell you a suitable animal; if you do well with it, this is good publicity for the breeder, besides which you will probably buy more of his stock in the future. The breeder will know the temperament, and the expected adult type and performance expectations of the family. Indeed he will almost certainly be able to show you adult relatives of the pony that you have chosen. Most breeders love to show prospective purchasers their stock, but do write or telephone first to make an appointment.

Unless you have previous experience of colts, it is better to buy a gelding or a filly. A colt will need to be kept alone once he is more than a year old, and he will probably become more difficult to handle as he grows older.

Aston Tinkerbell qualifying for Olympia at the Welsh Pony and Cob Show at Northleach, 1993. Tinkerbell was bought as a yearling from her breeder and has been with the author for sixteen years.

Buying at a sale

Another option would be to visit the annual sales which most breed societies hold – although bidding at an auction is probably not to be recommended to the newcomer! As an old hand at this, the author can reveal that even experienced buyers get very nervous about the whole thing, and that even they can end up paying far more than they expected for a pony they hadn't even intended to buy!

Once you have decided you really do want to buy at a sale, you should start by getting a copy of the auctioneers' catalogue as soon as you see the sale advertised. Most sales are advertised both locally and in *Horse and Hound*. The novice should not attempt to buy at a local sale, but should stick to the ones organised by the societies. The quality of animals at these sales is mostly much better than at local sales. Some vendors welcome prospective purchasers to view the pony at home before the sale, though usually you have to wait for the actual sale for the opportunity to buy.

Sometimes a description such as 'quiet to ride' is given: if later you find it to be untrue, then you can return the animal to the auctioneer. If, however, you find when you get the animal home that it has a defect such as a scar, or splint, or curb that you failed to notice before, you will have no redress. It is therefore most important to examine a potential purchase very carefully. Be sure that you see the registration papers, which will be lodged with the auctioneers and will be available for inspection at the sale.

If you decide to bid, you must first ensure that you have made arrangements to pay. This usually means that your bank must ring up the auctioneers' bankers (the details will be in the catalogue) well before the sale, and confirm that you have the necessary funds in your account to enable them to take a cheque from you. You can of course pay in cash. Do not expect to be able to write out a cheque without making arrangements beforehand. On the fall of the hammer, the pony becomes your property; you will need to provide your own headcollar and any other travelling gear, and of course will have to make transport arrangements. Most auctioneers will arrange temporary insurance to cover the journey home.

The private sale

If you are buying a ridden pony, you may find him in a stud or a sale, but he is more likely to be in a private home. It is very important that you satisfy yourself that he is suitable for your purposes; if it is your first purchase, you should take all the expert advice that you can get. If you are buying a lead-rein or first ridden pony, good temperament is vital.

Good ridden ponies – and potentially good ponies, for that matter – command very high prices these days. It is obviously cheaper to buy a young unproven pony, but then you may have to wait some time for him to come to his best; some of the larger breeds are at least six or seven before they are mature. Most ponies also go through an awkward 'teenage' phase at around two or three, when you may not be able to show them. They usually grow out of this ugly duckling stage however, and when they do become swans, it is all the more satisfying.

Buying the ridden pony

When buying a ridden pony, it is important to ask the following questions, as well as all the questions already suggested:

- Is he good to catch/handle/clip and shoe?
- Is he good to load? Does he travel well?
- Will he live alone (if you have no other ponies)? Can he be left on his own if others are taken away, to be ridden or for whatever purpose? Can he be ridden alone, and in company, without getting too strong or difficult?
- Is he good in traffic, and with large or noisy vehicles? There is often a great deal of noise and traffic on a showground.

- If you need to keep him out in the winter, you should ask if he is used to this.
- Has he ever suffered from sweet itch or laminitis?

It is always advisable to have any pony, but especially a ridden pony, vetted before you buy.

Be sure you obtain the breed society registration papers with your purchase, and that the papers do clearly apply to the pony. You should also ask if there are any other documents, such as a height certificate or registration papers for various competitions. You should re-register the pony in your own name as soon as possible. If you intend to compete in ridden classes where there is a height limit (such as NPS ridden classes) you should check that your chosen pony is under the height limit allowed.

So what do you look for?

The most important fact to remember is that if you want any success at all, your chosen pony must be a very good example of his breed. Each breed has important individual features – these are described in the separate breed chapters – and these must all be right. The pony should have good conformation (see page 22), and the overall picture should be pleasing. Movement should be naturally free, straight, and correct for his breed.

A nice head with a bold eye always attracts attention. If you can forgive a completely non-technical term, I am sure you will understand if I also say that he should have a 'smiley face'. A sour expression with laid-back ears is not going to get much attention from the judge – I am talking about the horse, but this advice also applies to the handler!

Colours and markings

Colour is a difficult subject, though good, strong, dark colour is easier to produce with a splendid shine which will glint in the sunlight. Markings should be correct for the breed. If white markings are allowed they look better if they are not too large, particularly on the face; white socks look better if they are

symmetrical, or nearly so. Be careful not to buy an animal with either coat or eye colour which is not allowed in your chosen breed. Acquired marks such as scars should not be accepted unless they are very small. Splints, windgalls and any such acquired faults are not allowed. A pony with sweet itch should be avoided as he will be rubbing off his mane and tail just when you want to show him.

Conformation

So what about his conformation? This is of great importance in the show animal. Small imperfections can be hidden by good presentation, but glaring conformational faults will ensure that you have no chance at all of being in the ribbons.

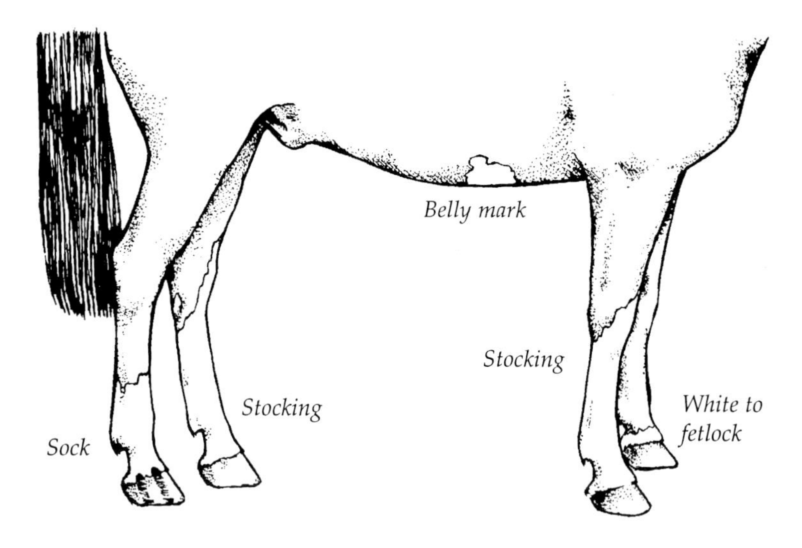

It is vital to start with a good basic framework: if the proportions are wrong – for example, if the back is too long compared to the length of neck or height of the animal – then the picture will be wrong. However, if the basic framework is correct, such problems as a lack of muscle on the neck or quarters can be put right with the correct work and feeding régime. If you make a habit of studying conformation and are consistent in your judgement, you can develop a good 'eye' and learn to recognise an animal of good make and shape.

Whilst each of our native breeds has certain special conformational requirements, there is a basic good shape which is to be looked for in every horse. Starting at the head, this is often what is noticed first. An attractive head with a large, bold eye is always appealing; if too much white shows around the eye, it is thought to indicate that the horse is mean or difficult. There is no real evidence to prove this, but subconsciously a judge may feel this to be true and so mark an animal down.

Welsh ponies should have a pretty head with a slightly dished face, whereas an Exmoor, for example, would have a larger head and a straighter face – though his head should not be in any way coarse or ugly. The head should be well set on, with enough room at the throat for him to flex onto his bridle; if he carries his head too low or too high it will affect his action

A good, basic shape

and his way of going. Avoid the tiny Welsh head with bulging eyes and no ears at all: you will find it extremely hard to keep a bridle or headcollar on this pony, quite apart from the fact that the move towards this type of head is not correct at all.

The mouth should be examined to check that the teeth meet evenly, and that one jaw does not protrude more than the other. The tongue should be a good fit for the mouth; if it is too large, it will affect the fitting of a bit. Never buy an animal which has signs of bit injury or mouth problems, as these are very difficult to correct.

The neck should be long enough for a good length of rein, but not too long to spoil the picture. It should be well muscled on top, but not overtopped with rolls of fat, which apart from being unsightly, prevent proper flexion of the neck. The neck should join the shoulder at the correct angle, and should be set on neither too high nor too low. The way a horse carries his head and neck can greatly contribute to that elusive factor known

Too long and weak in the back; lacking bone, lacking depth.

as 'presence'.

A well-sloped shoulder is important, as it allows plenty of movement in the front legs. It is also much more comfortable for the rider if he has something to sit behind on a ridden animal; an animal with a good shoulder will cover the ground better and therefore give a smoother ride. Care should also be taken not to allow too much fat to build up on the shoulder, as this will restrict movement.

Fat or flat withers can make saddle-fitting difficult for ridden ponies; moreover flat withers do sometimes go with straight shoulders, which should be avoided.

Most of our native breeds are expected to be round in the barrel and deep in the girth, with a strong back. It is important to have plenty of muscle on the back as a protruding backbone is not very appealing. The quarters, too, should be well muscled. There is an old saying about conformation, that a good pony should have the head of a duchess and the backside of a cook.

Sloping or weak hindquarters can indicate a weak back leg. If the middle section between the withers and the croup is too long, it is an indication of possible weakness. A good strong back, of the right length, does much to contribute towards good action.

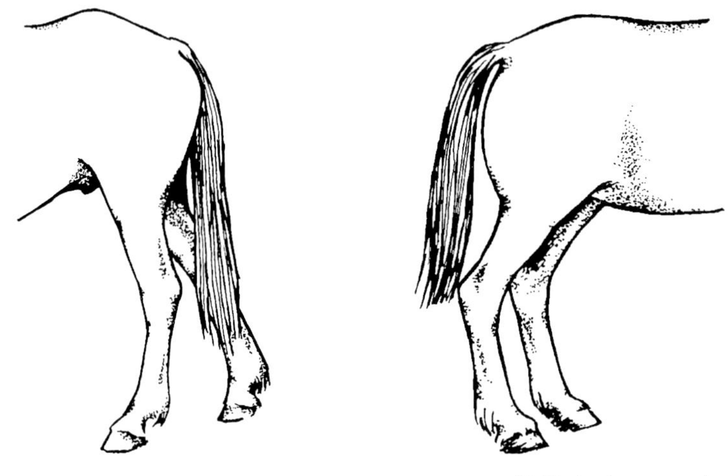

Poor hindquarters

Sickle hocks – a weakness

The stifle joint should not be noticeably higher than the elbow, and the underbelly line should run almost straight between these points. A belly which hangs down could indicate worms – though it could be just be full of grass. A line which shows along the side of the belly can be a sign of allergic coughing (broken wind/chronic obstructive pulmonary disease).

The bone and joints of the legs are to a certain extent determined by the breed, but in general, bone should be dense and flat. The pasterns should slope gently and be neither too upright, nor with too much slope; long pastern or cannon bones are a sign of weakness. The joints should not show any sign of puffiness or of windgalls, both of which indicate wear and tear.

The knee should be flat and should be in the middle of the leg – that is, when viewed from the front it should not be offset to the inside or outside and when viewed from the side it

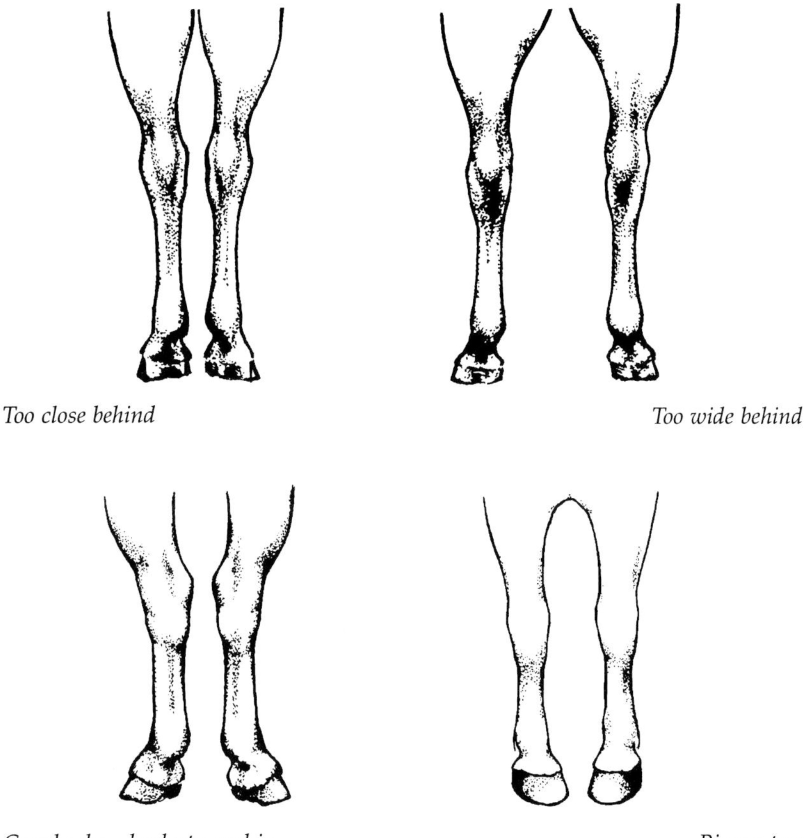

Too close behind

Too wide behind

Cow hocks – hocks turned in

Pigeon toes

should not appear to be pushed either forwards or backwards from the line of the leg. The front legs should not 'come out of the same hole' (be too close together); when viewed from the front they should be a pair, with the hoofs neither turned in nor out. The hind leg should be strong with a good hock. The hock and stifle should be at the correct angle for freedom of movement. The hind legs when viewed from behind should also be a pair, straight and set neither too close together nor too far apart. The hock should be strong and set at the correct angle (see diagrams) when viewed from the side.

In a native pony, the hooves will usually be of good quality, and indeed most natives can work happily without shoes: this will prevent the small, boxy hooves which ponies sometimes have. If a pony always wears shoes, its feet will not have the same opportunity to expand naturally as they would if it was unshod. If a pony has a slight weakness or unevenness this can often be corrected with good shoeing by an experienced farrier.

Movement

Movement should always be straight: dishing or plaiting are not acceptable, also the hind feet should follow exactly in the tracks of the front feet. The extent and type of movement is largely dictated by the breed, but generally speaking movement should be free and well away in front, and active behind. The walk is a four-beat pace, the hind feet following in the line of the front, but stepping further forward – that is, the print of the hind foot should fall a short distance in front of the print of the front foot. The trot should be active and springy, each diagonal pair of legs moving together; the hocks should be well under the pony to propel the movement forward. The canter is a three-time pace and shows best when the pony is well balanced and relaxed. The gallop should be free and should cover the ground, though a show gallop must also be controlled. When he jumps, the pony should round his body and fold his front legs beneath him.

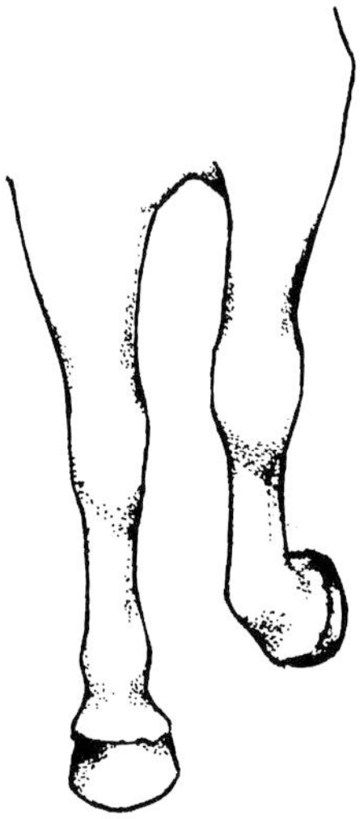

Dishing

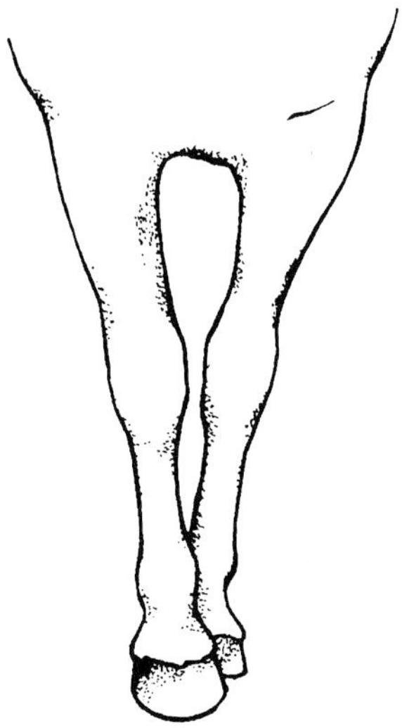

Plaiting

Presence

There is an elusive quality to be mentioned here, and that is one of presence. The pony who knows he is a star and always acts like it will always catch the judge's eye. This is largely something which an animal is either born with or not, but by always making sure that your pony feels well in himself and by keeping him happy with a varied routine, you can at least contribute to the overall picture.

CHAPTER TWO

Tips on Training

IF YOU intend to show your pony in hand it is important to start educating him when he is very young. It is always an excellent introduction for a young foal to be shown with its mother; it then has the chance to get used to the preparations; to travelling; to crowds and noises at shows; and to walking properly whilst being led. It is always good practice to handle ponies as much as possible, and as early on as possible to save work later; though don't worry if you buy a foal at weaning and he has not been handled, because he will soon learn!

THE FOAL

A foal walks naturally at his mother's side, and if you have a halter on him when you bring him from the field, he will soon learn to accept it. He needs to walk freely, and as quietly as possible by your side, and should always be encouraged to go in a straight line. The judge will be looking to see that he moves straight for the whole of his showing career so the sooner he learns, the better! He should be groomed regularly, and have his feet picked out and trimmed.

It is also important that he learns to stand quietly while his mother is led away from him, although keeping her in sight, as this will happen when she is trotted up in hand in front of the judge.

If you intend to participate in the winter foal shows, you will need to wean your foal reasonably early and to rug him up from about August onwards, depending on the weather. This will ensure that his coat does not grow too much, and with any luck it will also mean that he will stay reasonably clean. Young foals should not be bathed in cold weather.

When travelling a foal with its mother, the foal is usually left loose. Also travel the foal loose when he is first learning to travel alone, ensuring there is ample bedding for the first few times. After that he must learn to be tied up, though this should be a gradual process: first tie him up at home for operations such as grooming, then tie him in the lorry whilst it is standing still, and only after this travel him tied. Never tie any pony – and especially a youngster – directly to the ring but always to a piece of string which is then attached to the ring; thus if he pulls back for any reason he will break the string, and not his neck. As soon as he is travelling tied up, you should protect his legs with bandages or boots.

Never drag foals or young ponies round interminably from one show to another all season because they will quickly

Ballan Blodwen (by Sunwillow Ofenpass, out of Breaklands Gailforce) winning the overall supreme championship at the West Midlands Foal Show, 1991.

become sour. A few shows each year will teach them a great deal about life, but it is essential to have plenty of playtime in the field in between.

THE YOUNG PONY IN HAND

It is very important to practise everything that you are going to do at the show, well before you actually make your entry. However, always keep lessons short and regular. Your youngster should lead properly, by your side, not pulling in front or dragging behind. He should walk briskly and willingly. If you live in an area where the roads are quiet, you can take him out walking: this will practise leading, will get him used to different sights and sounds, and will help to build his muscles in a natural way. You must obviously have him under control, either with a bridle or a stout, well-fitting headcollar. Obviously it is better if he learns that he shouldn't jog, or buck, or shy; but he is only a baby and if he does any of these things it will not be counted against him, as long as he doesn't do it all the time, and providing the judge has a good opportunity to have a look at him when he is behaving himself.

Never use titbits as a training aid – you will just teach your pony to bite.

Early lessons

You must teach your pony to stand still and to stand up square, with his weight on all four feet, in preparation for standing him in front of the judge. He must learn to obey your voice, and should learn the command to 'stand', or 'stand up'; it is important to spend some time teaching this, because if he is moving about or you have to cajole him to stand still, the judge will not be able to see him properly. Once he is standing still and quietly, teach him to place his feet where you want them; this can be done by tapping a particular foot with your foot or a cane, and then praising the pony when he does as you ask. Some judges do not like to see this in the ring, and therefore it should be kept for training sessions at home. Welsh Cobs, and especially colts and stallions are taught to stand with their hind legs stretched out behind them, although nowadays this is not essential.

When the judge is standing on the offside of the pony, the legs should be in the following order: off fore; near fore; near hind; off hind. The legs should be reversed when the judge moves to the other side. The neck should be slightly stretched out, and the head held at the height which shows off your pony to its best advantage. He should also learn to walk obediently away when dismissed by the judge.

At this stage he must learn to 'get over' in the stable, and to be obedient in such matters as being caught.

If you have a colt to show, it will help if he sees other ponies often at home. If he is turned out regularly, preferably where he can see other horses, he will be less excited by them at a show. Colts should always be kept under control, and should never be allowed to misbehave lest they become difficult to handle. If you are an inexperienced handler, the best advice would always be to buy a filly.

Always act to quash bad behaviour before it gets out of hand. A young foal with its legs waving everywhere might look amusing, but when he is a big four-year-old, he will be downright dangerous if not discouraged. Do not get angry with him or lose your temper. Praise his good behaviour and deal with bad behaviour with a short, sharp 'No!'. Your voice is often more effective than a stick, although a schooling whip can be introduced in later training.

Further training

When you start to use a bit on your pony, you should first allow him just to stand in his stable for a short period of time each day with the bridle on; this will give him the chance to become accustomed to a bit. He can then gradually be led around wearing it, and eventually led from a lead-rein on a coupling which attaches to the bit rings.

Young animals should always be led from both sides so that their muscles and frame develop evenly; for the same reason they should also be led round in large circles on both reins. All too often youngsters are only led from the near side; also they always walk round on the right rein in the ring and as a result their bodies may develop unevenly which can cause problems when they are ridden.

All the preparations necessary for a show day should be practised often. It is no good waiting until the day of a show to give a pony his first bath, having found he has rolled in something disgusting. He might be as good as gold, but the chances are that he won't, and you will take much longer than usual to get ready and will make yourself late. You must also practise loading and unloading, and also just standing in the lorry or trailer.

It is important to keep a pony's feet trimmed so that he moves as well as possible. Besides, the judge will occasionally pick up a foot to look at the hoof, so it is obviously better if your pony is used to this. Judges may also sometimes take hold of the tail and hold it to one side in order to see the hind leg better. You should do this too, now and again in the course of grooming, otherwise your pony may kick out in surprise if it is done for the first time in the ring.

It may well be good for your youngster to have a 'show rehearsal' before his real debut, especially if he has not been shown as a foal. That is to say, you get him completely ready, just as for a show, load him up and travel him to a local event (it does not even need to be a 'showing' show, as long as there are other horses about) where you unload him and lead him around. Then if there are any problems, you will have time to iron them out before the big day.

From about the pony's second year you can start long-reining him as a training aid; basically, this is when the horse is driven in long-reins, the trainer being on foot. Some experts believe that this is a better training for a young horse than lungeing; possibly a combination of the two is the best solution. Do not attempt long-reining on the road until you have practised in the manège.

The adult pony in hand

For the more mature animal, a bit of practice at home will only be to the good, and if the pony has never been to a show before, then a rehearsal is bound to be useful. If you are showing a strong stallion, make sure you are fit enough to run round a big ring with him. You can muscle him up and get him fit by lungeing, or by walking out in hand or by long-reining. Some stallions are ridden or driven at home to develop the right condition for showing.

The brood mare should learn to run up and to stand, in just the same way as described for youngstock, if she has not been shown before. She should be separated from the foal for a few minutes occasionally, as will happen in the ring (although the foal will stay in sight). If she is broken to ride and is neither too old or unsound, she may well benefit from a little steady, gentle exercise up until the last month or so before foaling; this will keep her muscles and system generally in good order. Exercise

Gredington Calon Lan, standing up beautifully in hand. He is a Welsh Section A stallion (1985) by Revel Janus out of Gredington Judith, bred by Mrs S. Tyrell-Kenyon and exhibited by C. J. Tibbey.

could resume when the foal is about a month old, though beware of too much exercise as this may cause the mare's milk to dry up.

THE RIDDEN PONY

Were you to buy a 'ready-made' ridden pony, all that should be necessary is to get to know him at home, and to practise your show a few times before you actually get to the ringside. With a young unbroken pony, however, you will need to spend some considerable time schooling and training before he will be ready to be ridden at a show. If you have no experience of breaking and schooling, it is far better to employ a professional to do this for you. However, if you feel you can do this work yourself, please do remember that you should never cut corners. Horses do not forget a bad experience. Take things slowly, and both you and your pony will benefit in the end. It is very important to teach him good manners from the outset, and to insist on them always. It is no good letting him just wander off when you get on him at home, and then expect him to stand still for the judge at a show.

The ridden pony should be obedient and well balanced, and able to perform all transitions smoothly. He should stand still when being mounted, especially if he is to be ridden by the judge. The judge is most likely to ride at a breed show, but he may well do so at some other shows and it will not always tell you in the schedule. Your pony must therefore be used to other people riding him, too. Occasionally the judge is an adult, whilst your pony is only used to the weight of children, so do let an adult come and ride the pony occasionally for practice. All the native ponies are capable of carrying an adult, although they should not be regularly schooled by an adult if they are intended as a child's pony because this will make them used to stronger aids than a child will give.

It is important to teach him to walk off promptly and briskly when asked to do so. If he has been reluctant to leave the line-up, you should let him know discreetly, when the last pony is just about to finish, that you have a stick; you can then just tap him behind the girth as the previous competitor is saluting. Hopefully after doing this a few times he will walk forward when you ask, without resistance.

The walk is a very important pace. A pony should be taught to stride out well, without jogging; the rider should maintain a gentle but definite rein contact. Practise coming down from canter through trot, to walk, as you will do when going round the ring with the other competitors and also when doing your solo performance. You should ask your pony to trot, and if he is young or green he can trot for several strides to get the pace established. Bring him down to walk then, by closing your legs and hands; he should go as soon as possible into a rhythmical, forward-going walk. Far too many competitors are so relieved to have finished that part of their performance that they just collapse into a dishevelled walk, possibly even on a loose rein – just at the moment when the judge is having a final look!

It is better not to practise your show in its entirety too often, because an intelligent pony will start to 'learn' it and will anticipate changes of pace, and this can have an overall messy effect. Instead, you might practise the various transitions in different orders. It is also important that you do other things besides schooling; thus when you are hacking out, for example, you can practise your walk and trot and the transitions between them.

It is always a good idea to have taken your pony to one or more shows before he actually competes, to accustom him to the sights and sounds of the showground. He should be ridden in company as often as possible – when there are fifteen or twenty other ponies cantering in a class, most young ponies find this very exciting, and if it is his first time in company, he will find it doubly exciting. Some ponies object at first to strangers getting close to their tail, but they do have to get used to this. There will always be the occasion when there is a huge class in a tiny ring.

You must also 'teach' your pony to gallop. Although this is the favourite pace of most ponies, especially when you put them in the field on a frosty day, your ridden pony will need to learn a 'show' gallop. That is, he should go forward from canter to gallop with a definite change of pace, lengthening his stride and lowering his frame not necessarily with too much extra speed. He should also pull up obediently at the next corner, coming back smoothly to canter.

The working hunter pony

The working hunter pony will be going in the ring both in company and individually, just as the ridden pony does, but he will also need to have plenty of jumping experience. Our working ponies jump show jumps and cross-country fences as well as working hunter fences, particularly when they are learning their trade. Hunting is the very best way to make a pony bold at his fences, so if you live in an area where you can go hunting, make enquiries and take him along! Having said that you need to practise, on the other hand it is very bad to do too much schooling with a young pony. Most importantly, he needs variety in his practice sessions, not to go over the same two or three jumps at home every day, since the more different obstacles he sees, the less likely it is that he will be surprised in the ring. And he will learn far more by jumping lots of different small fences than by jumping the same big plain fences again and again – thus your practice fences can be anything up to six inches lower than the expected competition height.

Clear-round show jumping is another valuable experience, particularly as sometimes you will get one or two show-jumping-type fences in a worker course. Walls are a particular favourite – whenever did you see a red wooden wall when you were out hunting? Yet there they are in many courses!

Whilst the novice pony can jump his fences from a trot, your ultimate aim should be to complete the whole course at a good hunting pace, that is, a strong, forward-going, but controlled canter. You want your pony to approach his fences boldly, without hesitating or attempting to run out. He should jump cleanly, and then get away and back into his canter rhythm as quickly as possible. The experienced pony will do a flying change of leg when changing direction in the course, though it

Coppice Drummer, a Shetland gelding (1987) by Glenfall Excelsior out of Chatsworth Dolly Vera, bred and exhibited by Mrs S. Gibson, ridden by Emma Williams. Here he is competing in the working hunter class at the Three Counties Show in 1993.

is quite acceptable to put in one or two strides of trot to change legs. Agility can be improved by jumping small grids, and a small cross-country course will help your horse to gain confidence.

The most usual reasons for bad jumping or refusing are lack of training; pain, caused by badly fitting saddlery or an injury; bad presentation, bad riding, or lack of determination by the rider; or just plain overfacing. If you are having problems with jumping, but cannot recognise any of the faults above as applying to you, your best course of action would be to have some lessons with a professional trainer.

CHAPTER THREE

Equipment for the Show Animal

IF YOU already have ponies, then you will probably have most of the equipment that you need. If you are a 'first time' pony owner, then do not panic! Apart from essential daily care equipment, such as grooming kit, headcollar and so on, you can gather your other equipment gradually, as you do more showing.

Some items, such as leather tack, can be purchased second-hand. Second-hand saddles should be carefully checked for correct fit.

Do not ever compromise safety for the sake of saving money. For example, a cheap, badly fitting rug will rub your pony and spoil his coat.

THE FOAL

Unless you intend to do the winter shows, or your foal is ill, you will not need any rugs until he is into his second year. However, it is useful to have a small cotton rug to put on when he is ready for a show. This helps him become accustomed to wearing a rug, and it will keep him clean. It is debatable whether or not a young foal should wear boots or leg bandages when travelling; we usually start to use them when the pony starts travelling tied up. You will also need tail bandages, do take spare ones to put on at the show in case he gets one dirty. Even though a native pony does not have its tail pulled, it will

Leather slip for youngstock.

still look better flattened down, and it will need protecting whilst travelling.

Foals are shown in either a white rope or webbing halter or a fine leather foal-slip. Make sure that your lead-rope is long enough, so that if he should rear or suddenly pull away – as foals often do – you will not be obliged to let him go or be pulled over. (See the individual breed chapters for any specific requirements.)

THE YOUNG PONY IN HAND

Rugs

As your pony gets older you will need to acquire some suitable rugs. For example, if you intend showing him the following showing season, you will need to start rugging him up in January or February to ensure a good coat for the early shows. This may also include using a New Zealand rug in the field, so that he does not miss his stable rugs; it will also save you hours of work every evening scraping the mud off! There are many different types of rug on the market, and in these days of cross-surcingles you can safely buy a rug which is a bit too big, so that your youngster will grow into it; as long as it isn't enormous, tight surcingles should stop it from slipping. Always use a cotton sheet next to the coat; if this is changed about once a week it will help with grease removal and keep the coat lying flat.

As show animals need to be bathed fairly often, it is a good idea to have a towelling rug or one of the new thermal ones, to put on him after bathing to help him dry quickly. You may also find a woollen quarter-sheet useful – even in Britain there can be some very cold summer days which can make his coat stand on end if he gets cold in the collecting ring. Finally a waterproof sheet of some kind is invaluable. It is important that you practise putting these garments on him at home; if you start trying to put a waterproof on a young pony in windy, rainy weather on a strange showground, he might be forgiven for raising an objection.

Boots and bandages

By this time he will be wearing boots or bandages to travel in, and you may also like to use boots for lungeing. It is always better to lunge with a proper cavesson, lunge-rein and whip. By the third year you will undoubtedly be wanting to use a roller and side reins, especially if you intend to break him to ride.

Toys

On the subject of equipment for youngsters, I would like to make a mention of toys – yes, I did say toys! If your pony has to spend any great length of time in this stable, even native ponies develop such vices as crib-biting and chewing, and by providing suitable toys you can help prevent this. There are specialist items on the market, but a large plastic bottle secured to a length of plaited binder twine, is one which my ponies seem to favour. Other items might include a ball either secured by string or loose in the manger if you use one, or a tyre for a larger animal though this must be high enough so there is no possible chance of him getting his leg through it. I have one filly who plays for hours with an old towel draped over her stable door – she pulls it off and puts it back on endlessly until she misses and drops it over the outside of the door; hopefully some kind human then joins in the game and puts it back!

Stable and field equipment

Feeding bowls, mangers and any other stable fitting must be checked for sharp edges, also for spaces where a young pony might get a leg caught. Bowls and buckets which are not secured must have their handles removed. If you do not have a proper manger, do not use a haynet; although it is rather more wasteful to feed hay on the floor, it is infinitely better than finding your pony caught up in the haynet with a broken leg.

It is also important to check your field carefully if it has not been used for youngsters before. Foals can get through an extremely small space, and the smaller native breeds such as Dartmoors and Shetlands are often expert escapologists! In general, barbed wire and wire netting are not safe fencing materials for any horse.

Look carefully at your horsebox or trailer and check that your pony cannot get under or through the partitions, and that there are no spaces where a very small foot might get stuck.

These safety precautions are particularly important with a show animal as you will want at all costs to avoid injuries which may leave a scar or a lump.

Tack

As your pony grows up you will need to review the tack that you use in the ring. There is nothing worse than someone being dragged round the ring by a two- or three-year-old colt wearing only a halter, completely out of control and determined to demonstrate to every female on the showground that he is all man! Colts should always be adequately bitted, and indeed most show regulations require this: as a yearling, an in-hand bridle with a rubber straight-bar snaffle should be enough, especially for the smaller breeds, but as he gets older, if you intend to keep him entire you should invest in a horseshoe stallion bit and use it in conjunction with his in-hand bridle. Make sure that the bridle is right for the pony: a Welsh Section A or B, for example, needs a fine neat bridle with a stitched

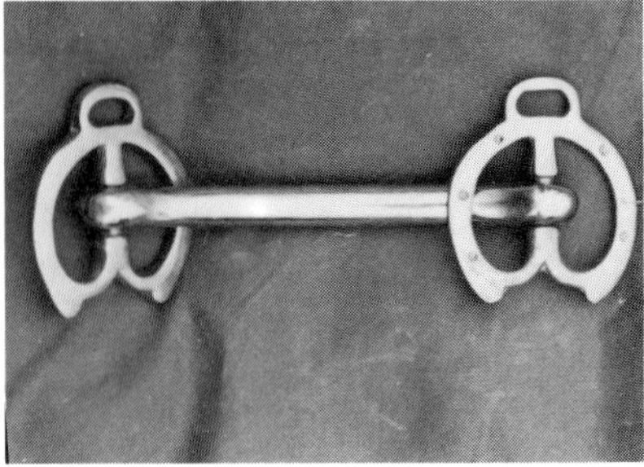

Above: Stallion bit. Left: Stallion bridle.

noseband; the Section D cob, however, requires an altogether more sturdy bridle – although this should not be so heavy as to spoil his head. If you use a bridle, use a lead-rein as described for the adult pony (see opposite).

Fillies are shown in either a webbing or rope halter or a neat bridle. (See also the recommendations given under the individual breeds.)

THE ADULT PONY IN HAND

The adult pony will need to have a full set of rugs, including at least two stable rugs so that he can have a clean one when he is bathed. He will also need two or three cotton sheets for wearing underneath his other rugs, and a New Zealand for playtime. Woollen and waterproof quarter-sheets are useful, as for the youngster.

Stallions are always shown in a bridle and adequate bit, and can also be shown in 'stallion tack': this consists of a leather roller, crupper and side-reins to the bridle. Some judges will ask competitors to remove the tack, except the bridle, believing that the crupper and side-reins influence the action and outline of the pony – as indeed they do. Mares can be shown in a halter or bridle, and brood mares in a double bridle. If you are showing

This picture shows stallion tack complete with roller, crupper and side-reins.

your ridden pony in hand, it is acceptable to show him in his ridden double or snaffle bridle.

The lead-rein can be either leather or white webbing, and should be attached to a coupling either of leather or brass chain, which divides into two, each side being attached to one bit ring. If you do not have a bit, the lead-rein should be attached to the noseband. There is often a brass ring on in-hand bridles for this purpose.

THE RIDDEN PONY

Rugs

Rugs are a part of life for of most ridden ponies. These animals will probably be clipped in the winter if in work and will therefore be quite used to being rugged up. Our own ponies have a rest from September to around February, when they are just roughed off without any rugs. When they come back into work it is too late to clip them and still get a good summer coat, so we rely on rugging them up and hurrying the change of coat. If you use this method you will also need a sweat rug or a thermal rug as long, sweaty native coats can take a long time to dry in the winter, and this can lead to your pony catching a chill.

Bridles

We have 'best' bridles and 'work' bridles, so that our showing tack will last a long time. Some people ride their ponies at home in a general-purpose saddle too, because these are more comfortable for the rider, and then use a show saddle in the ring. This is a luxury, however, and not a necessity.

Novice ponies should be ridden in a snaffle bridle and plain noseband. Open ponies can be ridden either in a pelham or a double bridle, though it is still quite acceptable to use a snaffle if that is what your pony goes best in. Nowadays, if a pony does not like the two bits of a double bridle or his mouth is really too small, you can buy a bit which has just one mouthpiece, either jointed or straight, but with the sides constructed to make it look like a double bridle (see photograph below). This provides a useful and neat compromise. It is referred to by different names, but often just called a showing bit. Bits should always be stainless steel.

Pelhams and double bridles should have two reins; roundings are not acceptable. However, split reins are allowed on a pelham for a small child. These are usually made up specially, and consist of two reins at the bit but which are joined together approximately half way from the bit to the hand, thus becoming

Double bridle with Weymouth bits.

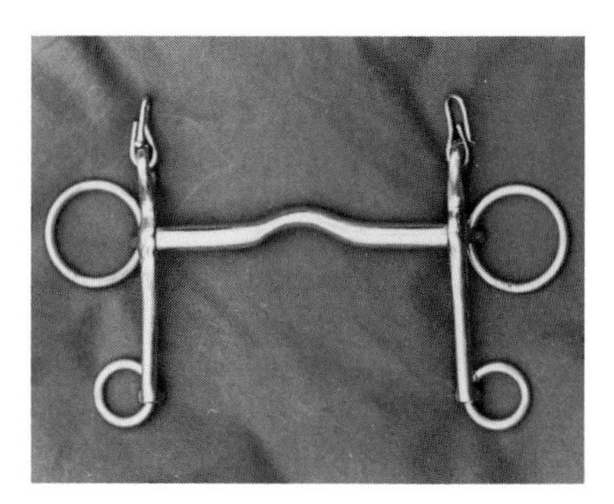

Showing bit.

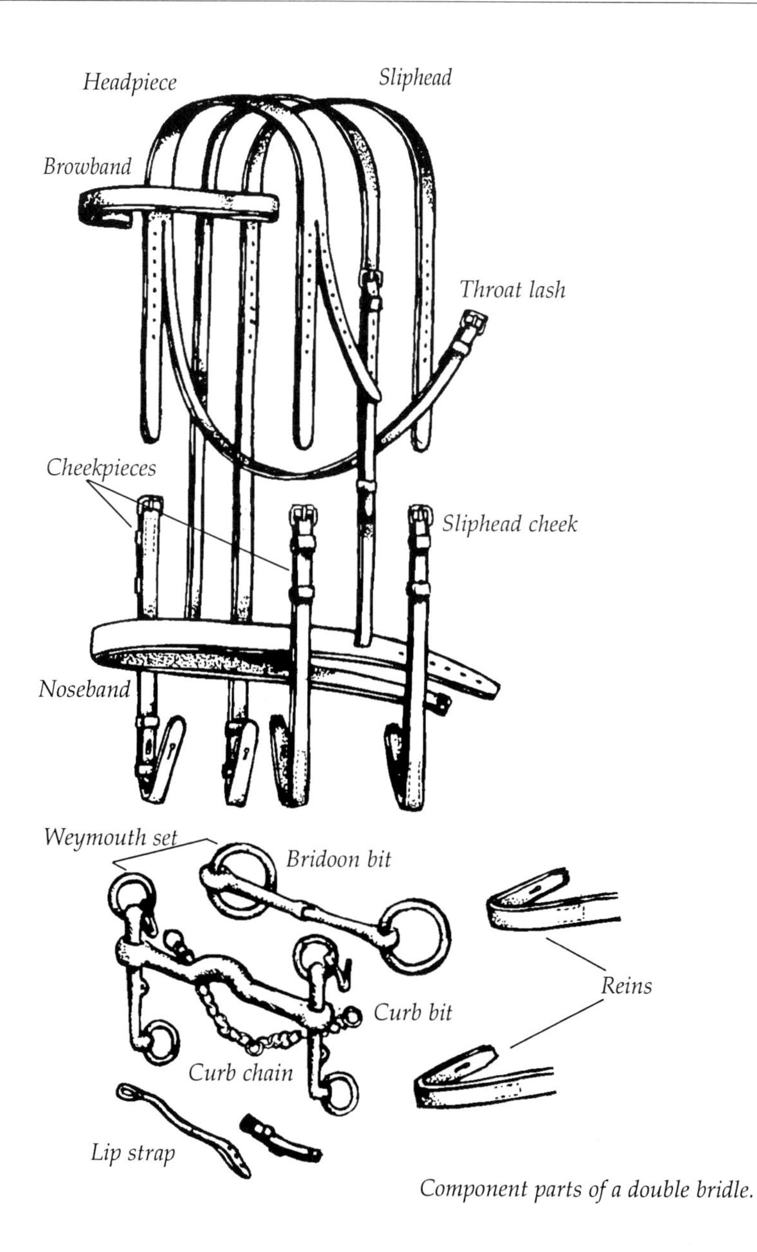

Component parts of a double bridle.

only one rein in the child's hand. The top rein can be plaited (leather) or ribbed for extra grip; you can also use a rein with rubber on the inside. Orange rubber reins are not correct. The width of the reins should be appropriate for the weight of the bridle; and if they are too long, they should be shortened, as flapping reins do not help to make a neat picture.

The bridle should be of a weight appropriate to the breed and

Drop noseband *Cavesson noseband*

Grakle noseband *Flash noseband*

size of the pony. It should be plain, although a rolled or stitched cavesson noseband is suitable for smaller ponies; ridden ponies wear only a straightforward cavesson noseband. Cobs and large breeds look good in a hunting type of bridle with a plain flat noseband.

Working hunter ponies are also permitted to wear a drop, a flash or a Grakle noseband, and a running or standing martingale. Any bit is acceptable, although a pony presented in a gag or a tight martingale will probably lose marks. Neither workers nor any other ridden pony wear any kind of boots or bandages when competing.

Saddles

Your saddle should be of fairly straight cut in order to show off the pony's shoulder. Smaller ponies can be shown in a flat,

This noseband is too low and too big, which gives the impression that the pony has a coarse head.

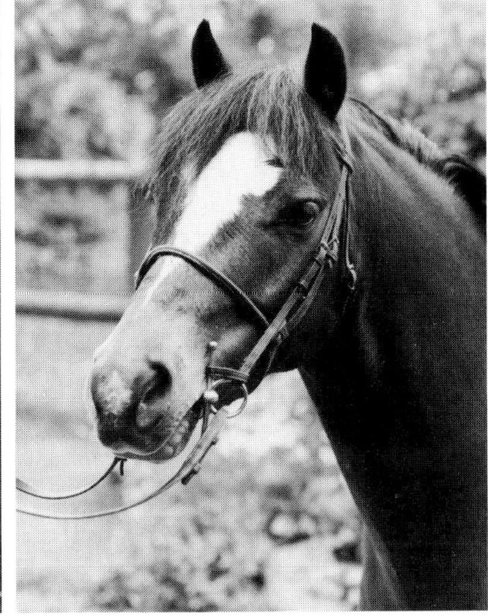

This bridle is far too small and light for this pony. He needs wider leather and a flat noseband (see cover and page 119).

straight-cut show saddle, although larger animals look best in a 'working hunter' type saddle. The saddle should be large enough for the judge, if you are planning to enter classes where the judge rides and you should also be prepared to supply another pair of stirrups and leathers if yours are likely to be too short or too small.

Stirrup leathers should be reasonably narrow, and not so long that the spare end hangs way down the pony's side. Irons should be stainless steel, and children can use safety irons; black rubber treads are useful.

With any saddle it is important that it sits behind the shoulder so that it does not impair movement. You can also choose a saddle to 'help' conformation: for example, if your pony has a long back you can 'shorten' him a bit by using a saddle with a slightly bigger seat and/or using a dark numnah which protrudes a little at the back. If his back is too short, use as small a saddle as you can get away with. One important point which is often missed when fitting saddles is that the gullet should always be wide enough to avoid any pressure whatsoever on the spine. Saddles are usually dark leather, but they can also be (dark) suede or have suede knee patches. Synthetic saddles are

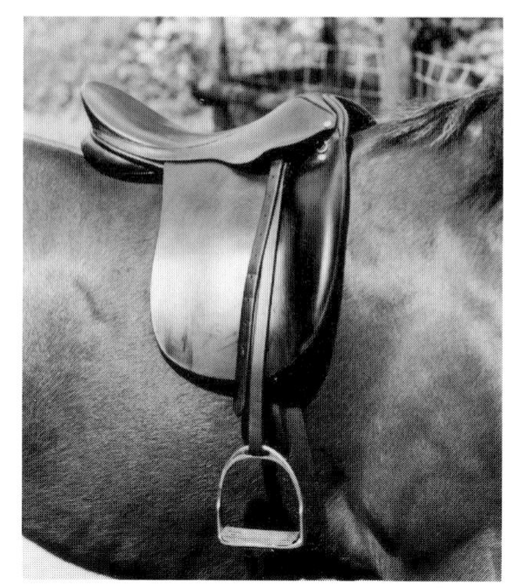

A good saddle, with a cut-back head and straight panel. The shoulder is completely free to move properly and fully.

not suitable for showing. If your saddle tends to slip it is acceptable to use a small sheepskin numnah, as long as it is largely hidden by the saddle, or a chamois leather. You should not use a large numnah or saddle cloth of any kind. All your tack should

This saddle is too forward cut and therefore hides the pony's shoulder. Also, the reins are too long.

be plain and discreet – for example, coloured browbands are not allowed.

Many owners of native ponies find it very difficult to get a saddle to fit the wide, flat back of the pony. If your saddle fits but slips forward, one solution is to ask your saddler to fit point straps. These run from the point of the saddle tree and in effect become the front girth strap, and this holds the front of the saddle down more firmly. Do not attempt to use a crupper, or a breastplate, or any other such item. The exception to this can be to use a crupper on Shetland ponies ridden by small children, but even so, it always looks better without.

All tack should be dark leather: never use synthetic items.

Chapter Four

What to Wear

THE HANDLER is part of the overall picture, so never think you can get away with wearing the clothes that you wore to get the pony ready! Men usually wear trousers and a tweed or plain jacket, or a dark suit with a shirt and tie. If the weather is warm, the jacket can be left off. A waistcoat is useful for both men and women; for one thing, if you are not wearing a jacket it will help to keep your tie in place. If it is very wet, an overcoat or waterproof jacket can be worn. Footwear is to a certain extent dependent on the conditions underfoot, and the speed at which the handler will need to run. It is no good wearing your best, stiff, shiny boots if you have to run up a big strong cob – you would be better with some tidy running shoes. Men in bowler hats usually provide good audience entertainment when they try to run and keep their hat on in a high wind! Make sure that you can run and keep your hat on.

Lady handlers should wear either trousers, of a plain, quiet colour, or something like culottes, which are easy to run in. Again, footwear is dependent on other factors, and hats are not really practical, although some ladies wear a neat headscarf. Never wear anything too bright or which flaps too much, as it will detract attention from your pony. A small discreet buttonhole is quite acceptable although not essential, but one which looks as if you have shares in a florist's shop will only make you look ridiculous.

In-hand handlers should carry a cane, either leather-covered

The immaculate turn out of pony, rider and handler all contribute to a really delightful picture. Nappa Meadowsweet (five years), by Nappa Country Boy, out of Seedhill Peaseblossom, owned by Mr and Mrs H. Richardson and ridden by their daughter Holly (aged six) winning the Novice Mini Championship at the Ponies UK summer show.

or plain. Sometimes with a stallion it is necessary to carry a short schooling whip. Gloves are optional, although they will of course be useful if your pony is strong.

Riders should wear tweed jackets in all classes, with a shirt and tie. Stocks can be worn in working hunter pony classes. Jodhpurs or breeches should be fawn or cream. Younger riders wear black or brown short boots; older riders wear long, black leather boots, with or without spurs, depending on the rules of the class. Do not wear a large buttonhole. Gloves should match the rest of your outfit, and a stick (if carried) must comply with individual breed society or national rules. Most shows now require the wearing of a skull cap which meets the appropriate British Standard in design, with a properly fastened chin strap. Skull caps should be covered with a stretch velvet cover to match your jacket.

A good example of smart presentation. Mrs J. Webb exhibiting her own Exmoor stallion Siskin, a five-year-old, by Hawkwell Cock Robin, out of Hazel.

Leading-rein handlers can look very smart if they take care to match their outfit to the colour of the pony and the costume of the rider. Do remember, however, that you will have to run in this outfit, so be sure that you can! You should also bear in mind that this is not a fashion show: your motto should always be 'neat and discreet'. Tons of make-up (presumably this only applies to ladies) is not necessary. There also seems to be a trend for adorning a child's hair with enough ribbons to make the rosettes for another show: please, one ribbon is enough!

Some shows require your groom to be wearing a hat when he or she comes into the ring; but whatever the case may be, grooms should be neatly and quietly dressed – shorts and skimpy tops do not really fit the bill. Moreover sandals or canvas beach shoes are actually very dangerous around horses – it really is better to suffer your smart clothes on a hot day for the duration of the class, than to leave your toes behind on the showground as you leave for hospital!

All your showing clothes should be regularly dry cleaned (or washed). It could well cause problems if you arrive at the next show and find your clothes in a dirty heap in the corner of the lorry where they have been since the last time – and I speak as one who knows!

Chapter Five

Preparations and Stable Management

IT IS IMPORTANT to have your pony in the right condition before you show him. If he is not fat enough, he will not look right; too fat, and he will not be fit enough for the rigours of competition and will probably not move as well as he might otherwise. There is a fashion nowadays for youngstock to be extremely large, with cresty necks and huge bodies. However, this puts a strain on the joints and the heart and will only cause problems later. Mares who have been very overweight are sometimes difficult to get in foal, and animals which are required for riding may be plagued with leg problems or laminitis. Ideally, the pony should be well covered but without excess fat, especially around the shoulders. His coat should be shiny and his eyes bright.

Hoof care and shoeing

A pony's feet should always be kept properly trimmed even if he is not shod, and this should be done by a qualified farrier. A pony's action and balance can be adversely affected by long or uneven feet. There is no need at all to shoe the smaller native breeds, particularly if they do little or no road work, but it is still most important to keep the feet in good condition.

If the pony is to be shod, the weight of the shoes should be appropriate to the size of the pony. The heavier the shoe, the higher it will encourage the pony's action to be, and in fact this can be used to advantage, for example for a Welsh Cob whose action might be thought to be too low or 'showy' – a heavier shoe will encourage him to move with a more suitably high action. However, there are weight limits for shoes laid down by some of the breed societies, and you should check this; besides, a good farrier can do much to improve your pony's action. The smaller breeds can wear lightweight plates, which will not affect the action at all.

Some ridden ponies have shoes which can take studs, or which have small permanent studs; this can be particularly useful for working hunter ponies. Studs used to be put in the outside-edge only of the hind shoe, but modern research shows that this can unbalance the pony and cause leg problems. It is now recommended that a second stud is put on the inside edge as well, to ensure that the foot is level.

The hooves should be kept in the best condition possible. There are a number of supplements on the market which can be added to the horse's feed to improve hoof condition and quality; and you should also apply hoof oil regularly. Cracks or splits in the hoof wall can be treated by rubbing well with Cornucrescine, a proprietary ointment which has been used for many years to improve hoof growth. Chestnuts should be kept neatly trimmed – the farrier will do this for you.

Feeding native ponies

It is essential that the show animal has plenty of oil in his diet – through linseed or vegetable oil and suchlike (see below) – and that he is allowed some time out in the field grazing every day, even if he is generally kept stabled. In particular this will help to keep him in the right frame of mind. There are many 'non-heating' mixes and nuts available nowadays which will keep your pony in good condition without making him too lively; though if you have the opposite problem and he is not lively enough, you can give him the old favourite, oats. If he is particularly dull or slow, you should of course check that he is not ill in any way.

Feeding is a complex subject, well covered in a number of

other books, but some simple rules are useful for the novice horse owner – and there may also be some tips for the more experienced!

The most important basic rules are:

- Feed little and often to mimic the horse's natural pattern when grazing.
- Feed only the best quality forage that you can find.
- Do not rely solely on grazing for all your pony's nutritional needs.
- Do feed mostly roughage with enough concentrates for the pony's condition and the work he will be required to do.
- Alter feeds gradually. Do not make sudden changes.
- Weigh your usual feed and mark the scoop, so you know how much you are feeding by weight, not by volume.
- Show animals should have plenty of oil in their diet. This can easily be sunflower oil, bought from the supermarket. Adding 0.1 litres of oil to a feed is the energy equivalent of 0.3 kilograms of oats, but without the heating potential of the oats.
- Ensure that the teeth are checked and that a suitable worming programme is carried out.

Good quality hay is important for show animals. Hay (or equivalent bulk forage such as haylage) should be fed at the rate of 70 per cent hay to 30 per cent concentrates, though this can be increased to 50/50 per cent for stallions. If good hay is not available, you can feed HorseHage or haylage, available either in small prepacked bales or increasingly in larger bales from farmers; however, both of these are usually higher in protein than hay, so you would need to feed a lower percentage of concentrates, particularly to ponies. HorseHage might be too rich for many smaller native ponies. If your pony has any tendency to cough, even good hay should be soaked.

It is important to provide adequate salt in the diet if your pony is travelling and being shown, especially in hot weather. A useful pick-me-up in hot weather is a bucket of water mixed with sugar-beet liquid.

Herbs are very useful in the producing of show animals. Fenugreek is unrivalled for putting on condition and for encouraging a fussy feeder, and its high oil content also puts a good shine on the coat. Nettle and kelp (seaweed) are both good coat conditioners. A handful of rosemary, covered with boiling water, soaked for a few minutes and then strained and cooled, makes a good mane and tail conditioner which is supposed to improve hair growth. It should be tipped on and left to dry naturally. If your pony has white hairs, possibly from an old injury, you can dye these with henna powder of an appropriate colour. Follow the instructions on the packet for dyeing human grey hair.

Certain herbs are extemely effective for calming nervous or highly strung animals (and their owners!); either buy a proprietary mix, or try chamomile tea – a pint of tea at double the strength of the packet instructions can be tipped over the evening feed each day. You should not strain out the flowers, and if you use tea bags, you will need to open them up and tip out the flowers onto the feed. If you try a proprietary mix and it doesn't seem to work, it is worth trying another one as they all have slightly different prescriptions, and different herbs suit different horses.

If your horse has to be stabled for any length of time, he will appreciate some carrots or even some cut long grass. However, do not feed grass cuttings from the mower.

It is widely believed that the quality of the water a horse drinks can affect his coat. Soft water certainly gives people soft shiny hair, so it may well do the same for horses. You could save rainwater if you live in an area of particularly hard water.

Feeding when travelling

It is very important to remember that horses easily become dehydrated when travelling to shows. If your pony has sweated whilst in the box, he should be offered electrolytes in his water.

In an emergency, electrolytes are available in paste form for administration by mouth, with a syringe. Some horses will not drink 'strange' water, so you should take some with you from home, if he is fussy. Water should be offered frequently even in colder weather.

If the journey is long or you expect to have your pony standing in the box for long periods of time at the showground, you should cut down on his concentrate ration to avoid digestive and other upsets. The best food for travelling is lots of good hay. If it is even slightly dusty and you have no alternative, it should be well soaked. Some people do feed concentrates whilst at a show, but native ponies really do not need this and will not lose condition if offered plenty of hay.

Fitness and exercise

Your pony will need to have a certain level of fitness, even if he is only to be shown in hand. If he is active, just the exercise he takes in the field should be enough; otherwise it can be gained by walking him in hand. Older ponies can be lunged, but take care not to overdo the lungeing and risk straining the joints.

The ridden pony will need to be quite fit. If he is in a big class in a big ring he will be going round for some considerable time and he will also need sufficient energy to do his individual show without sweating or puffing too much. If he is fit, he will have enough energy for the whole day. Fitness is difficult to judge, because the amount of work needed varies considerably between different animals. As a vague rule of thumb, if you can take your pony out for an hour's hack or do an hour's schooling without him sweating too much or being too distressed, then he has about the right degree of fitness for a show. Remember to vary his work so that he does not get bored.

Trimming and clipping

In general, the rule is not to trim or clip the native pony, but do look at the individual breed sections for specific requirements. If the mane is untidy, or falls to the wrong side or on both sides, it should be well brushed every day and then plaited over to the correct side. You should never cut a 'bridle pathway' in a native pony's mane, nor should you ever cut off any mane in the wither area. This is often done to non-native horses to help with putting on the bridle and saddle, but you will just have to arrange the long tresses of your native ponies as best you can.

Regular brushing of the mane or tail with a plastic curry comb can do a great deal to reduce the volume of hair! In principle tails should not be levelled off, although for a ridden pony it is better if the ends do not drag on the ground; a shorter length can be obtained by using a tail-thinning knife through the ends of the hair, and ideally the tail should end somewhere between the hock and the fetlock. Currently there seems to be a fashion amongst Welsh Cob owners to shorten the tail above the hock, presumably to make the ponies look more 'cobby'. Personally, I

Left: Tail in natural state. Right: The same tail after careful pulling and thinning. It will look even better after washing and bandaging.

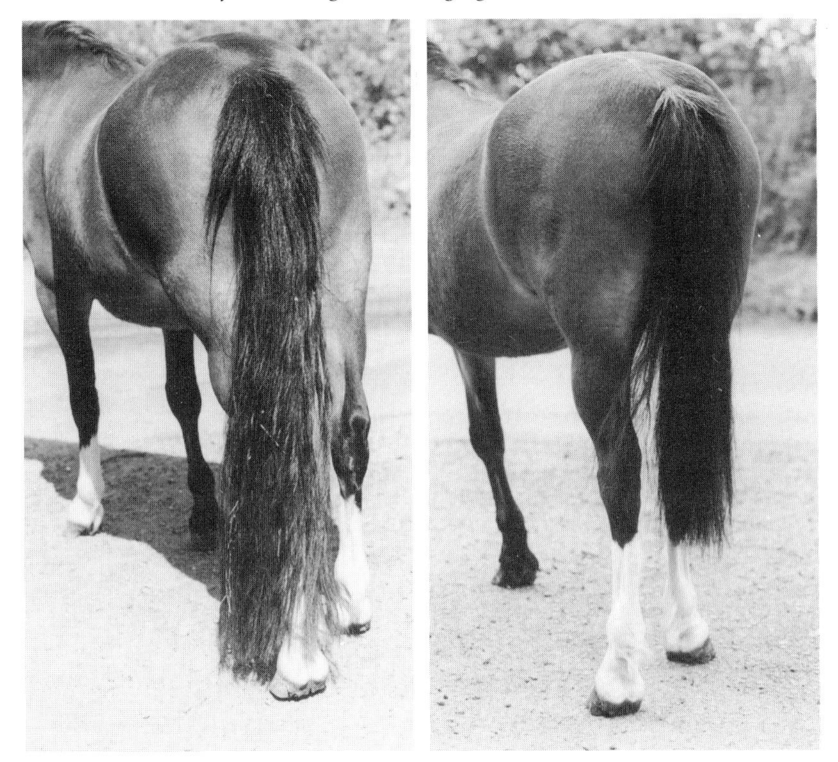

think it just looks as if it has been chewed by a cow or rubbed by the pony – and anyway this practice is against the spirit of the breed regulations.

Tail length can be used to 'improve' conformation: for example, if your pony has a long back, a tail nearer the hock will shorten him up; if he is short-coupled, a longer tail looks better. To keep him tidy, a few hairs can be carefully pulled out each side on the underneath of the dock, but this should be done so as not to be too noticeable. Don't ever use the clippers on a pony's tail for any reason at all.

If your breed regulations permit the trimming of hair under the jaw-line, do this with scissors or clippers, at least two weeks before the show, making sure that the effect is as natural as possible with the clipped or cut hair blending into the uncut hair at the edge of the jaw. The easiest way to do this is with small clippers, specially designed for the purpose. Whiskers should be left on. It is possible to remove the jaw-line hairs (and whiskers, if you really must) by singeing with a lighted taper, but most ponies are not too fond of this treatment, being naturally wary of a bonfire under their chin!

Ridden ponies can be clipped in the winter, and in fact for any pony doing real work, it is cruel not to do so. The best clip is probably a full clip, with the legs left on; it certainly looks tidier when growing out in the spring than does a trace or blanket clip.

Although to rug up a pony is strictly not a very native thing to do, it is essential in order to obtain a summer coat for the early shows. The average native pony knows it could well snow in April, and he is going to hang on to his coat so that he is prepared. Regular grooming will keep his new coat healthy and help remove the dead hair of the old coat. Stroking the pony all over with an old rubber glove on your hand is another good way to remove the old winter coat.

Washing and bathing

If you have a grey pony you may need to wash him all over at least once before his pre-show-day bath; white manes and tails

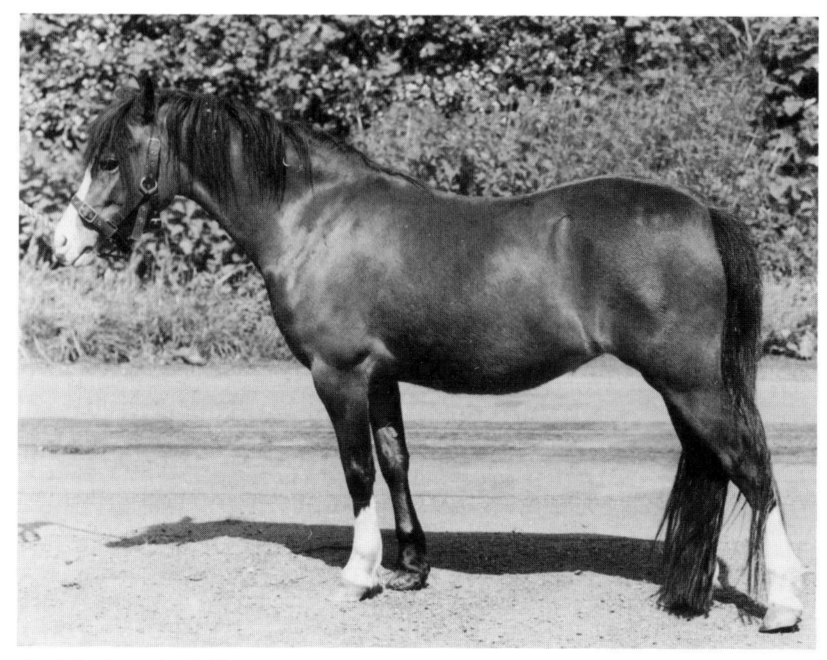

Straight from the field...

in particular can be very difficult to get white. We use a cheap family shampoo from the supermarket to wash our ponies, but if you have problems getting the mane and tail or socks really white, it could be worth trying a specialist product.

It is usually a good idea to set about washing and bathing your pony the day before a show, rather than on the day, although if he has white socks you might like to do those on the day. If the weather is very cold, it is better to wash only his mane, tail and legs and just wipe the rest over with a damp sponge followed by a rough towel. For a full bath, first make sure that you have everything to hand: this should include your buckets of warm water; shampoo (and any other products you need); conditioner for long manes and tails; towels; comb, scraper and water brush; sweat rug or towelling rug (and any other rug you may need afterwards); and tail and leg bandages and pads. We usually start behind the head, working backwards and leaving the head until last (if necessary). Hard, green, household soap is very good for stubborn stains and for white socks.

...ready for the show.

Be sure to rinse your pony very thoroughly, then scrape him down and blot the excess water with a towel. If it is cold, cover him with dry towels and rugs as you go. White socks can be washed and dried, and then bandaged to keep them clean; a layer of chalk can be applied before you bandage, for extra whiteness. There are several methods of getting the pony dry, from a special drying-room to trotting him up and down the yard – you will have to find out which works best for you. His tail should be bandaged, and if it is light-coloured, the unbandaged part can be enclosed in the leg from a pair of tights, bandaged in at the top to secure it. If he has an unruly mane, it can be plaited over. Very dirty ponies should wear a hood.

Tack and equipment

I hope it goes without saying that all your tack and equipment, and your clothes, should be clean and ready the day before a show. As one who sometimes cleans the tack in the collecting ring, could I respectfully suggest that you do as I say and not as I do! If you are new to showing, it really is important to check everything at least twice, following the sort of check list suggested on page 81.

Leather tack should be cleaned regularly with saddle soap, and oiled if it gets wet. Stainless steel bits and stirrups should be washed and dried; they should not need metal polish. White halters can be washed in the washing machine on a hot wash. Girths should be washed by hand, or put into a bag or an old pillowcase before being put into a washing machine. Brass is polished with a proprietary polish.

Chapter Six

Before the Show

MANY SHOWS now hold qualifying classes for mountain and moorland ponies, for championships held by the National Pony Society, Ponies UK and other smaller societies. Since the rules of the societies do vary from one year to another, it would be unwise to quote current rules: you must therefore apply to the individual society in plenty of time in order to register a pony, if the society requires this, and follow their instructions carefully. All the societies are helpful, and all are anxious to encourage newcomers to showing in whatever way they can. Not all affiliated classes require you to be registered to qualify – but do check first. (For addresses of the main societies, see page 124).

Entries

Shows vary tremendously in their rules for entries: some close entries weeks or even months before the show, some accept them on the day, and there is every variation in between. When you first receive a schedule for a show, make sure you note when entries close and post yours at least a week before that date. It is important to give all the information that is asked for, such as breed society numbers and so on; this information will probably be printed in a catalogue, and spectators and other competitors do like to read this.

Some shows will send your number through the post to you

before the day, usually together with a vehicle pass; others will ask you to collect your number on the day. If you are not sure whether you should have had documents from the show or not, you should ring the secretary and ask, a few days before the show day.

Check the rules in the schedule so that you know if your pony needs to show proof of vaccination. Some shows will not allow you on to the ground without inspecting the vaccination certificate for each pony; others don't ask for them at all.

Height limits

Almost all of the breed societies have a maximum permitted

Maximum height for age table

BREED	ADULT	2/3 YEAR OLD	YEARLING
Connemara	148cm	–	–
Dales	14.2hh	–	–
Dartmoor	12.2hh	–	–
Exmoor	Stallions 12.3hh Mares 12.2hh	– –	– –
Fell	14hh	–	–
Highland	14.2hh minimum 13hh	–	–
New Forest	14.2hh	–	–
Shetland	42"	40"	–
Welsh Section A	12hh	–	–
Welsh Section B/ Welsh Section C	13.2hh	13.1hh	12.3hh
Welsh Section D	14.2hh NPS rules; or no limit	–	–

Note: The Connemara Pony Society quotes measurements in centimetres; the Shetland Pony Studbook Society quotes theirs in inches; all others use hands.

height for adults – some also have height limits at various ages. Ponies are measured at some county and breed shows and all finalists in some of the National Pony Society competitions are required to produce a height certificate before the competition. Measurements are always taken either without shoes on or with an allowance for shoes. If a competition says that a height certificate is required, it refers to a Joint Measurement Scheme certificate. Measurement for this certificate is done by a designated veterinary surgeon at a proper measuring pad. For further details either contact your veterinary surgeon or the Joint Measurement Board office at the British Equestrian Centre, Stoneleigh, Warwickshire.

If you do intend to compete in competitions where there is a height restriction, you must check that your pony is under the required height before you enter. If you qualify for finals and then find your pony is over height you will be disqualified.

CHAPTER SEVEN

Show Day

IF YOU are new to showing, you should follow the check-list set out on page 81, and always pack up everything the night before. Add any personal items onto the list, but do use one – there is nothing more annoying than forgetting the bridle or, worse still, the pony! Make sure you leave ample time for loading the pony, particularly if he may be difficult; and if you need a food bucket to encourage him, or a lunge-line, then make sure it goes with you for use on the return journey. Even in warm weather it is best if a pony travels in at least a summer sheet as this will prevent his coat getting rubbed up the wrong way on the partition when he leans on it, and will also prevent his coat getting dusty on the journey there.

The most important thing is to arrive at the showground in plenty of time; therefore make sure that you know where the showground is, and allow an extra half-hour at least, in case you have to queue to get in, remembering that you travel more slowly with your trailer or lorry. Whether you entered in advance or intend to enter on the day, leave enough time to collect your numbers, and perhaps to queue at the secretary's office.

You will also need long enough to walk your in-hand pony round and to put the final polish on, or to 'work in' your ridden pony. In either case, this will stretch his legs from the journey, warm up his muscles, and settle him down if this is necessary. It is best to find a quiet corner of the collecting ring or the lorry park, but only experience will tell you how much work your pony needs before a class. Some ponies can come almost straight from the lorry to the ring, others need a considerable amount of time to get them settled. It can be useful to walk your pony around the showground so that anything unexpected such as 'bouncy castles' or go-kart racing can be seen and shied at well before the class. You should always also allow for the unexpected: for example, everyone who has ever shown a grey pony knows how it can liberally decorate itself with muck whilst travelling, given half a chance. Repairing the damage uses up valuable time.

On arrival it is advisable to ascertain the exact situation of the ring you will be competing in, and to check how far into the schedule the classes have progressed. From this information you will know roughly how long you have to get yourself and the pony ready. If you are in a ridden class, you will need to have a 'groom' standing ready at the ringside, to help you remove the saddle if necessary and brush off the saddle mark.

Final preparations

Any dirty marks the pony has collected during travelling, should first be washed off with plain water, then rubbed well with a rough towel; only use soap if it is really necessary, as it might be difficult to wash off. Ridden ponies with white socks can be ridden in with their bandages still on; these can be removed at the last minute. Chalk should be applied to white socks and to any patches which have remained stained on grey ponies; brush it in well so that it doesn't flake off should the judge run a hand over it. Coat gloss can be applied according to the instructions on the pack.

The mane and tail should be well brushed out, and either baby oil or coat gloss applied to make the hairs lie flat. If your pony has a really unruly mane you can try to tame it with products designed for human hair-styling, such as mousse or gel.

The feet should be picked out and hoof oil applied.

After the bridle or halter has been put on, rub baby oil onto the pony's nostrils and around the eyes. The practice of putting shoe polish or other blackening substances around the eyes is not to be recommended.

Finally, check that you have your number on and that you have put any necessary cards in your pocket, and then proceed to the ringside.

The in-hand class

The steward will call the competitors into the ring when the judge is ready for them. Do not walk in too close behind the pony in front – allow as much space as possible, though this is obviously dictated by the number of competitors in the class and the size of the ring. It is usual to walk round on the right rein (that is to say, clockwise). Use the whole ring: the judge cannot see the ponies properly if they walk in a tight circle

Gredington Calon Lan trotting out in hand after winning the Welsh Section A Male Championship at the Royal Welsh in 1993.

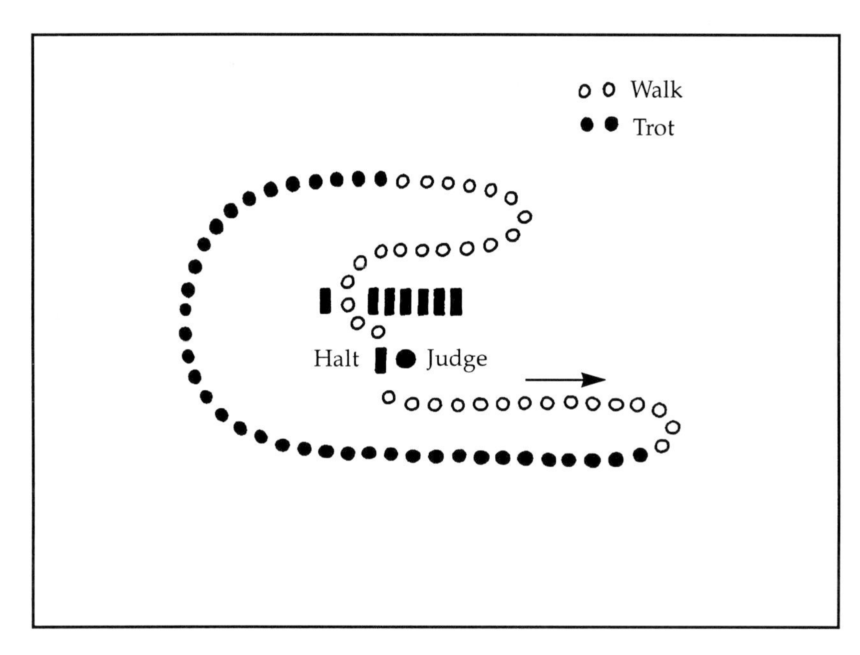

Pattern for the individual show when showing in hand.

around him/her. You may find that the class walks round together in this way for some time whilst the steward checks numbers and latecomers arrive.

Make sure that your pony walks on briskly, without pulling or dragging behind, and that you are concentrating on what is happening. At some point the steward will stop the class at a corner of the ring, and everyone should line up one behind the other (not too close!); each pony then trots out before the judge, one at a time. This is your chance to show your pony off – he should have learnt at home to trot smartly away when he is told, and so you would hope that he trots in a steady rhythm at your side. Ensure that you slow down soon enough to avoid crashing into the back of the line!

Once all the ponies have trotted up individually, the steward will ask everyone to walk on again. The judge will then be looking to make a preliminary selection. Keep your eye on the steward, and when you are called into line, go into the centre and line up, in the order that you were called.

Each pony will then be called out in turn to stand before the judge, and you will be asked to do an 'individual show':

- Walk away from the judge towards the edge of the ring.
- Turn right, and go into trot, trotting along the long side of the ring, and around the end of the ring. Return to walk.
- Retake your place in the line (see plan, page 71).

After each pony has done this part, the steward will signal the ponies to walk on again – if it is a very big ring, competitors probably will now walk in a smaller circle than before. The final places are then called, and the ponies lined up again; just occasionally the judge might change some placings at this time. The rosettes are then presented. A man wearing a hat should remove it when accepting a prize and thanking the judge.

It is most important to smile and thank the judge, whatever your feelings about your placing. Good manners are vital – remember there is always another day and another judge. I am sure that every supreme champion has been out of the ribbons at other times; I know all of mine have!

The class is then dismissed, and the prizewinners do a lap of honour, at trot, around the outside of the ring. The other competitors should make their way directly to the exit at walk.

The ridden class

Ponies should enter the ring at walk on the right rein. Always leave as large a space as possible between you and the next pony, and use the whole ring without cutting corners. Make sure that your pony is walking briskly but calmly, and remember to relax – and smile! Watch the steward for the signal to trot on. If you then find that you are 'stuck' behind a slower-moving pony, it is quite acceptable to overtake and to move to a space further on, or to circle behind you to find room. It is not, however, acceptable to trot around the middle of the ring inside the rest of the class, nor should you trot on the inside of another competitor thus obscuring him from the judge's view for any

Verwood Roger winning the supreme ridden title at Olympia, 1990. He is a Welsh Section D stallion by Dewid Meredith out of Hendre Tegwen, bred by Miss E. Salter and exhibited by Mrs C. Large.

length of time.

There will almost certainly be one particular side of the ring where the judge has decided he will watch the ponies trot. This is the time to concentrate and to ensure that your pony is going freely and easily. At some point the steward will give the signal to canter. If you have any doubts about your ability to get the pony to strike off on the correct leg, make sure you start your canter in a corner behind the judge so that you have time to correct possible mistakes, hopefully without being seen. Canter steadily, it is not a race. In some classes the steward may signal the competitors to gallop on along one side of the ring, and then it is important to leave enough space between you and the person in front. If you have done your homework, your pony should gallop on obediently and should come smoothly back to canter when you ask him at the next corner. However, most horses find galloping in company to be very exciting, and there may even be one who 'bolts', so this is a time to have your wits about you and to make sure that you are in control.

The steward will then give a signal to walk. Do not just collapse into walk, because the judge is now making a preliminary selection: you should walk on smartly, keeping your eye on the steward. When called into line, you should nod to acknowledge the steward, walk into line, and stand wherever you are placed.

Each pony will then stand out in turn in front of the judge, who will look more closely at its conformation, and then ask the rider to do an individual show. Some judges will ask for a specific pattern of show, telling you where to walk and where to trot and so on; if he does not, the following sort of pattern would be acceptable:

Suggested individual show for ridden classes.

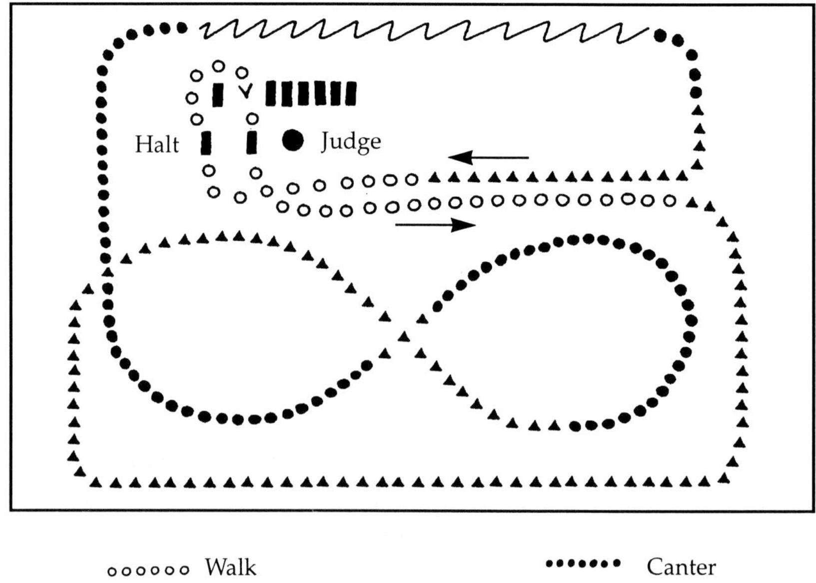

oooooo Walk   ••••••• Canter

▲▲▲▲▲▲▲ Trot   Gallop

- Walk away to the ringside, turning right at the edge of the ring.
- Trot on, trotting along the long side of the ring, turn right again at the end, and right again so you are going in front of the line of ponies.
- Then turn across the diagonal, which should take you directly in front of the judge, and go to the ringside, taking the left rein.

- Go into canter, and canter a small circle on the left rein, using half of the area between the line of ponies and the ringside. As you come to the centre, use a few strides of trot to change the rein, and then circle on the right rein. This time you should carry on along the side of the ring and past the line of ponies.
- As you get to the long side of the ring again, you should gallop on along the long side, pulling up to canter and then to trot, back in front of the line, and finally to walk.
- Walk to the judge.
- Halt squarely, and offer a salute. This is usually done by putting the reins into the left hand, putting the right arm down by your side and slightly bowing the head. Men can slightly lift their hat. The judge will then thank you, and you should return to your place in the line.

Once all the ponies have given their individual shows, the judge may or may not ask for the saddles of some or all of the ponies to be removed. This is so that any conformational faults may be more clearly seen, and so that the judge can see how the animal moves without a rider on his back. Your groom should be ready to come into the ring as soon as the steward asks you to remove the saddle, taking care to avoid any competitor who may still be doing his individual show. The saddle should be taken off and placed well behind the line of ponies. The groom may then brush off the saddle mark and make any other minor grooming procedures which are necessary; he/she should then stand with the saddle, behind the line. This is not the time for loud conversation on the merits or faults of the opposition, nor indeed for anything else.

Each pony will then be asked to come out and stand before the judge; he may well ask its age and will then proceed to inspect it more closely. At this stage, do not speak unless you are spoken to and never, ever volunteer information, especially details of your pony and/or its past success. Try and ensure that the pony stands still and that you have his attention. It might help to rustle a sweet paper in your pocket, or if he is really fractious, to pick a very small bunch of grass and hold it out to him – although the practice of grabbing large handfuls of grass and throwing them about is not to be recommended! The judge will then ask you to trot the pony out in hand on his own: you should walk away, turn to your right and trot back in a straight line towards the judge, adjusting your course, if he or she does not step to one side as you approach – there are no extra marks for squashing the judges! You should keep trotting to the ringside and round behind the line of ponies, coming back to walk to take your place in the line.

Your groom should then replace the saddle and you should remount. Grooms then leave the ring, again taking care not to obstruct any other competitor. When everyone is remounted, the steward will signal the class to walk on. Stay in order, as you were lined up; you will probably walk in a smaller circle than before. Watch the steward for the signal that you are being called into line. Always smile and pat your pony, whether you agree with your placing or not. Everything which has been said before applies equally here: so smile, thank the judge for the rosette, and make sure that you always behave with dignity. If you are in a position to qualify for the finals of a competition and this requires the production of a card, make sure you have it to hand for the judge to sign.

Prizewinners usually do a lap of honour at canter, and in important classes, the winner may then go on alone to gallop. Other competitors leave the ring at walk, directly to the exit.

The working hunter pony class

In this class, competitors are first required to jump a course of rustic jumps. The height of the fences will depend on whether or not this is an affiliated qualifying class, held under the rules of one of the societies. (Please see the individual rules books for the height of fences relevant to your pony.) The fences may include such obstacles as a water trough or a stile, for example, and you should ensure that you know what to expect and have practised such obstacles at home. Competitors are allowed to walk the course on foot first, so that you can memorise the route and have a closer look at the fences. Each competitor will then jump round in turn. This may be in catalogue order or you may need to give your number to a ring steward.

After everyone has jumped, all those who jumped a clear round, will be called in and if it isn't too big a class, all those

Aston True Welshman and Emma Williams negotiating a working hunter course.

who were not eliminated will also be called; each competitor then gives a show as in a ridden class. The saddles may or may not be removed, but your groom should be standing ready.

These classes are judged on a marks system and the marks for your class will probably be displayed or at least be available at the secretary's office later in the day. It could well help you to look at these and see which areas you need to work on for a better mark next time. If you have had jumping problems, there might be an opportunity at a small show – having first obtained permission, of course! – to jump around the course again after the classes have finished.

Lead-rein and first ridden classes

It is very important to consult the rules of individual shows and affiliated societies with regard to height of pony and age of rider, because they vary from one society to another and from show to show. In lead-rein classes the pony is led by a handler on foot by means of a rein attached to the pony's noseband, and the format of the class is very much like an in-hand class. The 'leader' should walk by the pony's head, holding the rein in the left hand; the right hand should only be used if necessary to guide the pony. The pony should be a little distance away from the leader, to show that it is going quietly on its own and not being restrained in any way. The trot should be slow and gentle.

In first ridden, the ponies walk and trot together as for a normal ridden class, but do not canter. They are, however, allowed to canter in their individual show. There is often a requirement for ponies to be shown in a snaffle bridle in these classes, but not always – so do check the rules.

The championship

If you are lucky enough to be first or second in your class, you will be required to come into the ring again at the end of the classes, to be judged for a championship. The format will be a repeat of your class, but this time you will be against the winners of the other classes. It is considered bad manners not to appear for a championship, even if you feel that your pony has no chance.

Judges and judging

So who is the judge whose opinion you have asked regarding your treasured pony? Normally judges are people who have either shown or bred (or both) the type of pony which you are showing, for many years. They will have been through either the probationer scheme run by the two main societies, or an assessment day run by the breed society. Usually they are personalities well known in the world of pony showing long before they become a judge.

Often judges travel considerable distances to judge, giving up their time for very little reward. They do not get paid, though the larger shows will offer travelling costs and refreshment; at some smaller shows they are lucky to get a sandwich and a cup of coffee. They run the risk of being abused by irate exhibitors, and of being soaked to the skin or baked to a frazzle whilst they judge.

So what can we expect from the judge? At all times judging should be seen to be absolutely fair. Judges should not be swayed by a competitor's past form or by the fact that an exhibitor is a well-known professional. It is always best, too, if they can be seen to have a type which they prefer. If you know a judge likes chunky ponies and yours is on the fine side, for example, you can save an entry fee by not showing under that judge. Finally they should be consistent with their treatment of misbehaviour – if one ridden pony is moved down for bucking, then so should anyone else who does the same.

In mixed mountain and moorland classes, it is reasonable to expect the judge to know the difference between the various breeds. Possible exceptions are between a Fell and a Dales, where black ponies of these breeds can look similar, and between a Welsh Section B and a small New Forest.

You should also reasonably expect the judge to be watching the class carefully, and to be watching each exhibit's individual show. The judge who was chatting to the steward during a ridden competitor's show and then noticed the child standing in front of her and saluting and said, 'Oh, have you done your show then, dear?' should learn to concentrate on the job in hand. However, if this does happen to you, then I am afraid you will just have to grin and bear it as part of showing – and avoid that judge in future! The judge should not study the catalogue before or during the class, and should not ask competitors who they are, or what their pony is, or how it is bred. If judging is under the rules of a society, then judges should know the rules and enforce them.

Judges should always be polite and firm, but never too aloof. The judge who refuses to answer a polite enquiry from a competitor, after the class, is not doing his bit to improve showing generally and to encourage newcomers.

So what can the judge expect from you? You should always be punctual at the ringside, and come into the ring as soon as the class is called. You should be properly turned out and in control of your animal. You should obey the instructions of the steward, and be alert and concentrating on the job in hand.

You have to go into the ring with the attitude that you are going to accept the opinion of someone else, whether at the end of the day you consider that opinion to be right or wrong. There are always going to be days when you feel hard done by, and days when you feel that you have been lucky. This is what showing is about – the old saying that 'every dog has his day' applies to showing ponies, too: they usually all have 'their day' eventually.

If you find a judge who likes your pony, you can look out for him/her at other shows. However, do not be disappointed if you do not do so well another time. Although he or she likes your pony, there may be other competitors in the class whom the judge likes better on that particular day. The only class where the judging is not solely a matter of opinion is a working hunter class, where the marks are allotted partly on jumping, with faults for mistakes, and marks for performance and for conformation.

At the end of the day, remember – you are doing this for fun!

Show day checklist

For the pony

- Saddle and bridle, or bridle, or halter.
- Quarter-sheet and rain sheet.
- Spare rug (in case one gets wet). Spare bandages or boots, and spare tail bandages (so that you can put on a clean one between classes).
- Grooming-kit box, including brushes, comb, hoof oil, baby oil, coat gloss, chalk (if necessary), cloths. Fly repellent.
- Washing bucket, including shampoo or soap, water brush and towels.
- Haynet (and spare hay).
- Water bucket and enough water to last all day.
- First-aid kit. There is usually a veterinary surgeon on call at shows, but you should carry enough equipment to deal with small wounds. The following should suffice: skin-cleaning swabs; wound powder; wound dressing and bandages; Animalintex or similar poultice; cold pack (Tendoneze or similar); scissors; thermometer.
- Vaccination and height certificates (if required). Competition cards, if required for qualifying class.
- Stout sack or bucket and rubber gloves or fork for mucking out. Most shows now forbid mucking out onto the showground.

For yourself

- Clothes, including waterproofs (if you don't bring them, it is sure to rain).
- Boots, gloves and whip or stick. Hat (of the correct standard) and hat cover.
- Provisions. Not all shows have catering laid on.
- Passes and numbers, if they have been sent to you before the show.
- Map.
- The schedule.
- Camera for photos of your prize-winning pony.
- First-aid kit: this should include painkillers; wound swabs and dressings; and antihistamine cream. Chamomile tea bags are useful to calm you down. Sun lotion is a must in the summer (it can also be used on ponies with pink noses).
- A mobile phone is very useful in the case of a breakdown or serious problem – and also to convey the good news home when you win!
- Money.

Above all, do not forget the pony!

Groom's box for the ringside

- Small bucket or box to carry things in.
- Body brush.
- Comb.
- Cloth.

PART TWO

THE CONNEMARA PONY

THE CONNEMARA is an ancient breed from County Galway in Ireland which from time immemorial has both worked on the farms and provided harness power for the local people. Since the merchants of Galway traded with the Spanish, there is probably an infusion of Arab and Barb blood in the native Celtic pony.

The English Connemara Pony Society is the youngest of our native pony societies – it is less than fifty years since Cynthia Spottiswode first brought Connemara ponies to England from their native Ireland. The Spottiswodes were an Anglo-Irish family and Cynthia spent many of her childhood holidays in Connemara. The original Connemara Pony Breeders Society had been formed in Galway in 1923, when the first stud book was opened, and the first ponies to be brought to England were registered in this stud book.

In 1947 the first post-war National Pony Show included Connemaras in its schedule, although in mixed classes; it was to be the 1960s before pure-bred Connemara classes were first seen in England.

In 1953 the English society was reconstituted. By 1964 the decision had been made to inspect all two-year-old colts before they could be registered, and by the late seventies the Connemara was being hailed as a 'much-improved breed'. Since 1979 the society has published the stud book itself, together with the *Connemara Chronicle*, the society's annual journal.

Honeylake Baccarat, a Connemara gelding (1981) by Arrow Chevalier out of Holton Solitaire. Bred by Mrs E. Walker, exhibited by Julie Walker.

John Mead has been breeding well-known Connemara ponies at the Leam Stud since 1947; his *Leam Bobby Finn* was a most influential sire in recent years. As chairman of the English Connemara Pony Society from 1947 to 1982, the present-day Connemara enthusiast must owe much to him.

The society organises inspections of stallions and mares for the stud book which it also publishes. It also runs three shows, a performance awards scheme and a sales list.

Breed Standard

CHARACTERISTICS Good temperament; hardiness and staying power; intelligence and soundness; surefootedness and jumping ability; suitable for a child or an adult.

HEIGHT 133 - 148 cm.

COLOUR Grey, bay, black, brown, dun with occasional roan, chestnut, palomino and dark-eyed cream.

TYPE Compact, well-balanced riding type with depth,

substance and good heart-room, standing on short legs covering a lot of ground.

HEAD Well-balanced pony head of medium length, with good width between large, dark, kindly eyes. Pony ears, well-defined cheek bones, jaw relatively deep but not coarse.

FRONT Head well set on to neck. Chest not overloaded and neck not set on too low. Well-defined wither and good sloping shoulder giving a good length of rein.

BODY Deep with a strong back. Some length permissible, but should be well ribbed up with strong loins.

LIMBS Good length and strength in forearm, well-defined knees and short cannons with flat bone measuring 18-21cm. Elbows should be free, pasterns of medium length, feet well shaped of medium size, hard and level.

HINDQUARTERS Strong and muscular with some length, well-developed second thigh and strong, low-set hocks.

MOVEMENT Free and true without undue knee action, but active and covering the ground.

Presentation

Many Connemaras are performance ponies, and so are clipped during the winter. Most exhibits in any ridden class also seem to have pulled manes and tails, although often the show regulations do not permit this. The most sensible course of action is usually to compromise and 'tidy' the mane and tail whilst leaving it as natural as possible.

THE DALES PONY

THE DALES PONY is native to the upper dales of Tyne, Wear, Swale and Tees, and stems from the Pennine pony with infusion of Scotch Galloway, Norfolk Trotter (as in the Welsh Cob) and Wilson pony. There is also a belief that Spanish blood runs in the veins of these ponies, there being a strong tradition of trading in Iberian horses in their native area. Originally bred for the Pennine lead industry, they were famous for their weight-carrying abilities and their endurance.

Dales are excellent harness ponies, having been used for trotting and for all farm work. Their ancestors were probably used for chariot racing by the Romans, particularly the troops used to guard Hadrian's Wall.

Encouraged by the National Pony Society, a stud book was opened in 1898. Originally it was believed that Dales and Fell were two types of the same breed, which were given the name 'Brough Hill' ponies. In the early days of the stud book there was a certain amount of crossing of the breeds, usually by crossing Dales stallions with Fell mares, but the difference between the breeds was still recognisable. Then in 1916 the Dales Pony Improvement Society was established, and although there was still some crossing of the breeds up to 1948, each breed was also established separately.

With so many Dales ponies being used by the army in the two World Wars, by 1955 only four registered Dales ponies remained. In 1963, the society was reorganised as the Dales

Pony Society. A system of inspection was introduced, and quality mares which had lost their papers or were of unknown breeding were allowed to be registered in section D of the stud book. This allowed numbers to increase to around sixty by 1970. In 1981 the society was able to withdraw from the umbrella of the National Pony Society, and with the support of the Rare Breeds Survival Trust is now able to stand alone. All stallions are now licensed by the society and all foals are registered, free of charge, in their year of birth.

The Dales pony has a bold temperament, great presence and a very good trot. He is usually very surefooted and of an equable nature, not given to panic in difficult situations. They have energy, agility and much stamina. The breed has been shown under saddle for many years, being traditionally shown at the walk and trot only. The trot is an all-important pace and in-hand handlers should be prepared to sprint energetically to show their animal off to his best advantage.

The society holds spring and summer breed shows, a breed performance show, a performance points awards scheme, an annual pleasure ride, and a Dales pony driving rally.

Warren Lane Jupiter, a Dales gelding (1987) by Waterside William out of Lowbrook Dawn. Bred by C.W. Smith and exhibited by Mr and Mrs I. Graham.

Breed Standard

CHARACTERISTICS Tremendous stamina; iron constitution; high courage and great intelligence; also calm temperament and very surefooted.

HEIGHT Up to 14.2hh.

COLOUR Predominantly black with some brown, grey and bay; rarely roan.

TYPE Excellent harness ponies, having been used for trotting and for all farm work; the trot is an all-important pace. Famous for their weight-carrying abilities and their endurance.

HEAD Neat, showing no dish and broad between the eyes. Muzzle relatively small, no coarseness about the jaw and throat, and incurving pony ears. A long forelock, mane and tail of straight hair.

FRONT The muscular neck of ample length for a bold outlook, should be set into well-laid sloping shoulders. Short, well-developed forearms set square into a broad chest. Withers not too fine. Stallions should carry a well-arched crest.

BODY Short-coupled, with strong loins and well-sprung ribs.

LIMBS Cannons should display an average of 8-9in of flat, flinty bone with well-defined tendons. Pasterns should be of good length with flexible joints, the hooves large, round and open at the heels with well-defined frogs, and with ample silky, straight feather. Dales are renowned for the quality of their hard, well-shaped feet and legs with beautiful, flat dense bone.

HINDQUARTERS Lengthy and powerful with very muscular second thighs, above clean, broad flat hocks, well let down.

MOVEMENT Their action is straight and true, they are good movers, really using their knees and hocks for powerful drive. They are renowned for their very good trot.

Presentation

No trimming or plaiting is allowed. Although some ponies are still seen with traditional tail ribbons, this is discouraged. Manes and tails should be left full and flowing and the feather untouched. Youngstock can be shown in a white halter or leather slip. Brood mares are shown in a bridle or halter. Bridles for ridden animals should be medium weight with a flat noseband.

Rules of Registration

Ponies can only be accepted for registration through the Dales Pony Society; ponies entered in the stud book must have three generations of recorded breeding on both sides. Applications will only be accepted for ponies up to two years of age though exceptions to this rule will be considered by the Council.

Colts will be registered as follows: Colts eligible for stallion status must be by a registered, licensed stallion and out of a Section A Dales mare, and must display correct markings. All stallions are re-entered in the stud book when licensed. Stallions must be licensed from three years of age.

Colts out of a Section B, C or D mare, or mismarked colts out of a Section A mare, are not eligible for stallion status. These colts will be issued with a temporary certificate of eligibility for registration, and will be registered as geldings when castrated.

Mares, fillies and geldings will be registered as follows:

Section A: By a registered licensed stallion and out of either a Section A or a Section B mare, and displaying the correct height and markings.

Section B: By a registered and licensed stallion, and (a) out of a Section A or B mare, but displaying incorrect height or markings. (b) out of a Section C mare and correct in height, type and colour.

Section C: By a registered, licensed stallion and out of a Section D mare, and correct in type, height and colour.

Section D: Passed by inspection as being true to type, height and colour (closed 31/12/71).

THE DARTMOOR PONY

THE ORIGIN of the Dartmoor pony is lost in time, but there are references to small ponies in the area as far back as 1012. At the time of the Industrial Revolution, some Shetland blood was introduced to reduce the size of the moor ponies, for use in the mines. When the National Pony Society opened its stud book in 1899, there was a Dartmoor entry of five stallions and seventy-two mares. The description used at that time varies little from today's breed standard except in the matter of height, this being originally 14hh for stallions and 13.2hh for mares. It appears from historical documents that very few actually reached that height, although they were of course often ridden by full-grown men. There is a story that tells of the famous 'grey mare' of the old song 'Widdecombe Fair' being in fact a Dartmoor mare.

Almost all present-day Dartmoors trace back to one stallion known as *The Leat* who was a part-bred, by the Arab *Dwarka*. *The Leat* was eventually admitted to the stud book, even though he was not pure Dartmoor. He was owned by the first secretary of the Dartmoor Pony Society, which was established in 1924. Ponies were used on the moor for shepherding amongst other jobs, but perhaps their most unusual task was to escort prisoners from Princetown jail to work in the quarries. The prison bred Dartmoors and part-breds which were used up to the 1970s.

After the war, when ponies were no longer needed on the farms, the Dartmoor enjoyed an increase in popularity rather

Shilstone Rocks Snowbird by Shilstone Rocks D-Day out of Shilstone Rocks Snowfall. Exhibited by Mrs R. M. Taylor and Mr M. Ball.

than a decline. In their new role as children's ponies, they have been exported all over the world. Many new breeders appeared, often in other parts of the country. The ponies on the moor, however, did not fare so well, with annual drifts and many foals going straight to the petfood trade.

In 1988 and 1989, two schemes were set up to improve conditions and standards. The 'Moor' scheme was introduced to encourage Dartmoor farmers to use a good, selected stallion on unregistered (but pure) mares, whose offspring (female) could be upgraded to a supplementary register. It can only be hoped that these schemes will succeed and that there will be no more horror newspaper headlines about starving moor ponies. The ponies involved in these incidents were in fact for the most part not Dartmoor ponies, but rather 'ponies living on Dartmoor'. Only a small percentage of the ponies now living on the moor are true Dartmoors, the rest being crossbreds and other ponies belonging to local people.

In 1979 the Dartmoor Pony Society took over the task of registrations. The current rules for registration are to be found in the annual Dartmoor Diary, which is available from the society.

Special rosettes are given to registered ponies at various shows and a performance award scheme is run annually. Details of these are also available from the society.

Anyone who owns a Dartmoor pony will soon find out that they are bright characters, full of fun and extremely intelligent. They jump and drive and generally have the personality to enjoy everything they do. Being of sensible temperament they make good lead-rein and first ponies.

Breed Standard

HEIGHT Not exceeding 12.2hh.

COLOUR Bay, brown, black, grey, chestnut, roan. Piebalds and skewbalds are not allowed. Excessive white marking is discouraged.

HEAD Should be small, well set on and bloodlike, with the nostrils large and expanding, and the eyes bright, intelligent and prominent. The ears should be small, well formed, alert and neatly set. The throat and jaws should be fine and showing no sign of coarseness or throatiness.

NECK Strong, but not too heavy, and of medium length. Stallions should have a moderate crest.

SHOULDERS Good shoulders are most important. They should be well laid back and sloping, but not too fine at the withers.

BODY Of medium length and strong, well ribbed up and with a good depth of girth, giving plenty of heart-room.

LOIN AND HINDQUARTERS Strong and well covered with muscle. The hindquarters should be of medium length and neither level nor steeply sloping. The tail is well set up.

HIND LEG The hocks should be well let down with plenty of length from hip to hock, clean cut with plenty of bone below the joint. They should not be sickle- or cow-hocked.

FORELEG Should not be tied in at the elbows. The forearm should be muscular, and the knee fairly large and flat to the front. The cannon should be short with ample good, flat, flinty bone. The pasterns should be sloping, but not too long. The feet should be sound, tough and well shaped.

MOVEMENT Low, straight and free-flowing, yet without exaggeration.

GENERAL The mane and tail should be free and flowing. The Dartmoor is a good-looking riding pony, sturdily built yet with quality. In appearance and movement he might be compared to a scaled down version of a middleweight hunter.

Presentation

The Dartmoor is never clipped or trimmed. The exceptions to this are that full clipping is allowed for Olympia, also Dartmoor ponies that hunt are usually trace clipped. The Dartmoor is shown in a plain bridle, although a brass browband is permitted. Youngstock are shown in a leather slip, and brood mares are shown in a lightweight in-hand bridle. Two-year-old colts must be bitted.

THE EXMOOR PONY

THE EXMOOR has been roaming the moors of Devon and Somerset since ancient times, being mentioned in the Domesday book. The remoteness of their habitat not only gave them their hardy nature but also ensured that they are amongst the purest of our native breeds. As with most of the other native breeds, they were first registered in the Polo Pony Stud Book, the first registration being that of the colt *Snowflake* in 1892.

The Exmoor Pony Society was formed in 1921 by Earl Fortescue KCB and 148 ponies were registered by 1922, with the society having seventy members. As today, the Exmoor has always been the only pony breed to be branded, and although some of the old brand marks have died out, one of the oldest, the anchor, is still seen today. Numbers were severely depleted by the war, only forty-five mares surviving. By the seventies numbers were still perilously low and the breed was declared a rare breed. The Exmoor Pony Society undertook a census which showed that there were in fact only 500 Exmoor ponies worldwide. Even today numbers have only risen to around 800.

Although Exmoor ponies are bred in other parts of the country, the majority are still bred on the moor. In the autumn the mares and foals are rounded up for inspection; pure-bred foals are examined, and if accepted into the breed as typical specimens, they are then branded with their individual number on the near flank and the society's star and their herd number on the near shoulder. Exmoor ponies can often only be identified by these markings as they are not allowed to have any white hair whatsoever. The strict rules of the society have also ensured a greater degree of conformity than is seen with other breeds.

There have been a number of prominent Exmoors in the show ring in recent years. *Dunkery Buzzard 78/48* was rarely beaten in hand, and often took mixed mountain and moorland championships. *Redsyke* is another well-known performer, both under saddle and later as a brood mare.

It is absolutely imperative that Exmoors are shown in a completely natural state: no clipping, trimming or pulling whatsoever is allowed.

Breed Standard

HEIGHT Stallions and geldings, not exceeding 12.3hh; mares, not exceeding 12.2hh (at any age).

COAT Close, hard and bright in the summer. Dense and thick in the winter.

COLOUR Bay, brown or dun with black points; mealy colour on muzzle, round eyes and inside flanks; no white markings anywhere.

TYPE Definite 'pony' character; hard and strong; vigorous and alert; symmetrical in appearance; mealy muzzle and 'toad' eyes.

HEAD AND NECK Ears short, thick and pointed; clean-cut face; wide forehead; large eyes, wide apart and prominent (toad eyes); wide nostrils; mealy muzzle; clean throat; good length of rein.

SHOULDERS Clean, fine at the top, well laid back.

CHEST Deep and wide, between and behind forelegs. Ribs long, deep, well sprung and wide apart.

BACK Level; broad and level across the loins; tail set in neatly.

LEGS Clean and short, with neat, hard feet; forelegs straight, well apart and squarely set; hind legs well apart, neatly perpendicular from hock to fetlock, with point of hock in line with pelvis bone; wide curve from flank to hock joint; legs free in motion with no tendency to sweep or turn.

ACTION Straight and smooth, without exaggeration.

QUALITY Alert expression and general poise indicating balance and symmetry of movement. Fine clean bone.

Presentation

An Exmoor pony is a lovely colour to get ready for a show! However, it can be difficult to get a shine on his dense coat except in the height of summer. Youngstock are shown in halters. Adult ponies are usually shown in an in-hand bridle; this can have a brass browband, as can the ridden bridle.

The Exmoor Pony Society offers premiums to registered stallions, gives prizes at shows and keeps a list of registered ponies for sale. An annual show is held at Exford on the second Wednesday in August. Full details of registration and membership can be obtained from the society.

Winged Bowman, an Exmoor stallion (1983) by Hawkwell Quarme out of Knightoncombe Scorched Wing. Owned by Mrs S. Poulter. Note the clearly visible brand.

THE FELL PONY

THE FELL PONY SOCIETY was founded in 1893, and ponies have been registered since 1898; Her Majesty the Queen is the present patron. HRH the Duke of Edinburgh drives the Queen's own team of black Fells with great success. The breed today is one of the purest of the native breeds. Originally used as pack horses and for general farm work and by traders on the northern fells, today's Fell pony holds his own in showing classes and for riding, driving and any other job you can think of. Their docile temperament makes them ideal mounts for disabled riders.

Fell ponies are well known for their trotting ability. Trotting races used to be held on the Cumbrian fells, often on a marked course, of one mile on hard road. The Fell's well-known dense blue hooves needed no shoes for this competition. A few ponies are still bred in a semi-natural state in Cumbria, but like all the other natives, most are bred by enthusiasts who are scattered all over the country. It is interesting to note that the late authoress Beatrix Potter was a supporter of Fell ponies, as was King George V.

These hardy and versatile ponies really came to notice as ridden mountain and moorland ponies when *Lunesdale Lucky Lady* (shown on page 101) won the 1992 National Pony Society ridden championship at Olympia. This lovely mare proved that, when properly schooled, a Fell pony can hold its own against any of the more plentiful breeds. Some Fell riders make the mistake of letting their ponies go too much on the forehand and this spoils the impressive trot, which is there if the rider takes the trouble to encourage it. The pony should be ridden well up into his bridle, and encouraged to show his paces properly. Absolutely no clipping or trimming of any kind should be done, and emphasis is placed on good silky feathering which should extend from the back of the knee to the heels. Great importance is placed on good legs, with plenty of flat bone and good feet, the latter being round and open and consisting of the characteristic blue horn.

The Fell Pony Society has shown a good increase in membership lately; it holds an annual stallion and colt show in May and a breed show in August. There are also two performances each year, a southern show in Oxford, a pleasure ride, and the annual registered show and sale in the autumn.

Breed Standard

HEIGHT Not exceeding 14hh.

COLOUR Black, brown, bay or grey, preferably with no white markings, though a star or a little white on the hind feet is allowed.

MANE, TAIL AND FEATHERS Plenty of fine hair (coarse hair is objectionable). All the fine hair, except at the points of the heels, may be cast in summer. Mane and tail are left to grow long.

HEAD Small, well chiselled in outline, well set on, forehead broad, tapering to nose. Nostrils: large and expanding; the eyes prominent, bright, mild and intelligent. Ears: neatly set, well formed and small. Throat and jaws: fine, showing no sign of throatiness or coarseness.

NECK Of proportionate length, giving good length of rein, strong and not too heavy. Moderate crest in the case of a stallion.

SHOULDERS Most important, well laid back and sloping, not too fine at the withers, not loaded at the points; a good long

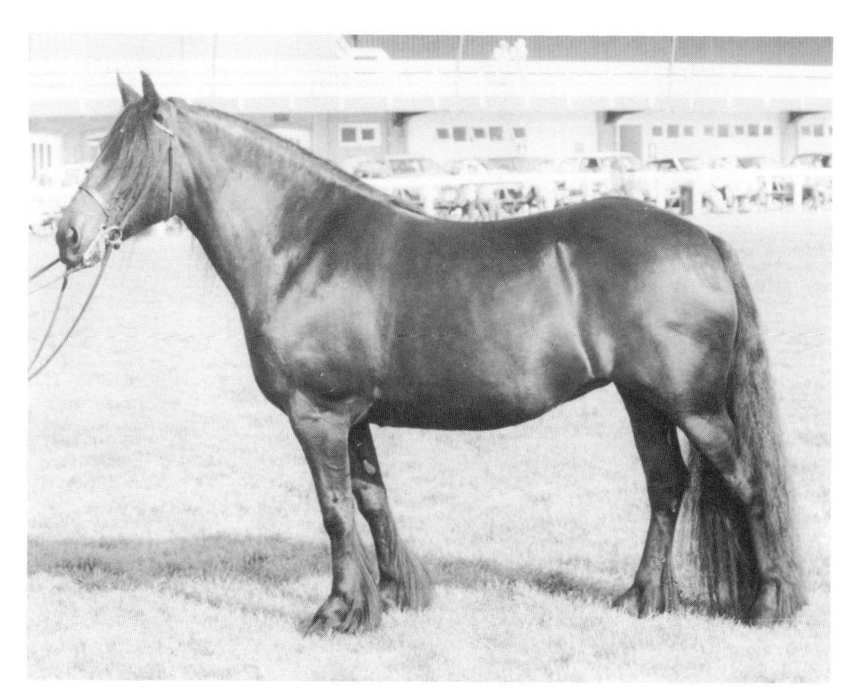

Lunesdale Lucky Lady, a Fell mare (1983) by Townend Flash out of Lunesdale Grey Dawn. Bred by Mr A. Moreland and exhibited by Mrs O. Briant. This mare is a previous winner of the supreme ridden title at Olympia.

shoulder blade, muscles well developed.

BODY Good strong back of good outline; muscular loins; deep carcase, and thick through heart; rounded ribcage (from shoulder to flank); short and well coupled. Hindquarters square and strong with tail well set on.

FEET, LEGS AND JOINTS Feet of good size, round and well formed, open at the heels with the characteristic blue horn; fair sloping pasterns, not too long.

FORELEGS Should be straight, well placed and not tied at the elbows. Big, well-formed knees; short cannon bone, plenty of good flat bone below the knee (8in at least). Great muscularity of arm.

HIND LEGS Good thighs and second thighs very muscular, hocks well let down and clean cut, plenty of bone below joint –

should not be sickle- or cow-hocked.

ACTION Walk, smart and true. Trot, well balanced all round with good knee and hock action, going well from the shoulder and flexing the hocks; not going wide or near behind. Should show great pace and endurance, bringing the hind legs well under the body when going.

GENERAL CHARACTER Constitutionally the Fell pony should be as hard as iron; it should show good pony characteristics with the unmistakable appearance of hardiness peculiar to mountain ponies. It should also have a lively and alert appearance; and great bone.

Presentation

The mane and tail should be full, as should the feather. Take care not to flatten the feather with tight bandaging – if boots are worn, slightly loose-fitting ones are better (as long as they are not so loose that they come off). Take care when buckling bridles not to trap the long jaw hairs. Youngstock are shown in a bridle or white rope halter. Older ponies should have a bridle of medium weight with a flat noseband. Some Fell ponies are shown with a brass browband.

THE HIGHLAND PONY

POSSIBLY THE STRONGEST and hardiest of the native breeds, the Highland pony has a long recorded history, including a number of pedigrees which go back to the 1880s. Robert Burns wrote in the 1780s of his 'Highland filly', and at about the same time Dr Samuel Johnson had made his famous Highland journey on the back of a pony. Carrying weights of up to twenty stone (110kg) up and down hills and living out all year in rough conditions has produced a modern-day pony of exceptional hardiness and strength, with an excellent, patient temperament. In the past there have been sub-types of the breed, including the rather lighter Western Isles pony, but none of these are now recognised by the breed society.

The support of our present queen for the breed is well known, both through Her Majesty's stud and through her patronage of the society. This royal association was begun by Queen Victoria, who started the Balmoral stud around 1850. Pedigrees have been kept since 1896 and the Highland Pony Society was formed in 1923. The stud book was never divided into sections so ponies of rather diverse type and height were crossed together in different ways to produce whatever size and build was required. Even today, registered ponies vary in size from 13hh to 14.2hh although all are generally strongly built. The society is working to breed ponies with bone and substance, with considerable success.

Ponies compete at the top in ridden and working hunter pony

Donald of Altnacriche, a cream dun Highland stallion (1988) by Duant of Glenmuick out of Nina of Altnacriche. Bred by G. Henschell and exhibited by Mr and Mrs McLauclin and Mrs Grant.

classes and make sensible, strong driving ponies. Ponies are still used on some Highland farms and are of course also still used for carrying deer. They are very economical to keep, and live out all the year round. Care should be taken not to overfeed a Highland pony, particularly when he is living on rich lowland grass. The colours of the Highland pony give testimony to his long history, being various shades of dun, brown-black and grey. Many show dark points, stripes on the neck and shoulders, eel stripe along the back and zebra stripes on the legs, another indication of ancient origins.

Breed Standard

HEIGHT 13hh to 14.2hh

MANE AND TAIL Hair should be long, silky and flowing, not coarse. Tail set fairly high and carried gaily.

COLOURS Various shades of dun: mouse, yellow, grey, cream, fox. Also grey, brown-black and occasionally bay and liver chestnut with silver mane and tail. Many ponies carry the dorsal eel stripe and many have zebra markings on their forelegs. Apart from a small star, white markings (blazes, socks etc.) are disliked and discouraged.

Stallions with white markings, other than a small star, are not eligible for registration.

HEAD Well carried, broad between alert and kindly eyes; short between eyes and muzzle; muzzle not pinched; nostrils wide.

FRONT Neck: strong, not short; good arched top-line; throat clean and not fleshy. Shoulders: well sloped. Withers pronounced.

BODY Compact; back with slight natural curve; chest deep; ribs well sprung.

QUARTERS Powerful; strong, well developed thigh and second thigh.

LEGS Flat, hard bone; forearm strong, knee broad; short cannon, pasterns oblique, not too short; well shaped, hard, dark hooves. Forearm placed well under the weight of the body; hocks clean and flat. Feather silky and not over-heavy, ending in a prominent tuft at the fetlock.

Presentation

Youngstock can be shown in a rope halter or leather slip. Ridden ponies should have a bridle of sufficient substance. Many in-hand handlers like to wear a kilt, or tartan trousers or skirt. This is not, however, essential and dress can be as for other breeds.

THE NEW FOREST PONY

THE ORIGINS OF the New Forest pony in the great Hampshire forest are uncertain, but a pony skeleton has been excavated and a decorated pot showing a pony, and these have been dated at around AD300. There are also records of a royal stud in medieval times, at Brockenhurst – and breeding ponies must have been far more profitable then than it is now, because the profits from this stud helped to build Beaulieu Abbey!

The New Forest was mixed with outside blood at various times in the past, as happened with other breeds. Possibly the most famous sire used on New Forest mares was *Marske,* who also sired the famous racehorse, *Eclipse.*

In the 1880s the Four Stallion Society was formed in order to try and improve the stock because it had been found that although there were a good number of useful mares, the stallions used were generally inferior. The reason for this was that most ponies ran out in the forest and so a stallion owner could not charge a fee, besides which there was also always the chance that the stallion might get injured or even killed. Any good colts were therefore kept at home or sold on.

The Society for the Improvement of New Forest Ponies was formed in 1901, the function of this society being to hold a stallion show, where premiums were allocated. At around this time, the Burley and District New Forest Pony and Cattle Society was formed to hold an annual show at Burley Manor Park; it also organised races for New Forest ponies. In 1905 the first show was held, which included mares, foals and youngstock; by 1906 there were three ridden classes. The first of these was for 'a registered New Forest pony suitable to carry a man to his work', and ponies in this class were expected to carry a stone in weight per hand. The other two classes were for 'ride and drive' ponies and for a 'child's hunter'. This society started the stud book. It also initiated the annual 'take your own line' three-mile point-to-point race across the forest which has been held every Boxing Day (with the exception of wartime) since then. In World War II, ponies living wild on the forest were fitted with luminous collars so that cars could see them in the blackout; they were not very successful, however, because they soon became muddy.

By 1935 it had been decided that ponies with the least 'outside' blood thrived best on the forest, and the stud book was then closed. In 1938 the two societies – the Improvement Society and the Burley Society – were amalgamated to form the New Forest Pony Breeding and Cattle Society.

Willoway Pipers Gold, a New Forest stallion (1983), by Peveril Peter Piper out of Tomatin Goldrush. A prolific winner under saddle, bred and exhibited by Mrs C. A. Large.

Although originally the height limit had been 12.3hh for mares and 14.2hh for stallions, market pressures forced the height limit for all ponies up to 14.2hh. After the war, New Forest ponies were exported all over the world. There are now breeding herds in many European countries and also in America, Australia and New Zealand.

The New Forest pony of today does every job for every member of the family. The stallions which nowadays are used on the forest must prove their hardiness by running on the open forest for at least one winter before they can be considered for final approval. They are also vetted for hereditary unsoundness at two and five years. At present some 2,500 ponies roam the 145 square miles of the forest; they are rounded up annually for the Beaulieu Road sales, which the society organises at Lyndhurst, when they are also recorded, wormed and those that are to be kept are branded. Any which may not winter well on the forest are removed. Each year the society also organises a performance competition, a stallion show and a summer show.

Breed Standard

HEIGHT The upper height limit is 14.2hh. There is no lower limit, but ponies are seldom under 12hh.

COLOUR New Forest ponies may be any colour except piebald, skewbald or cream with blue eyes. Bays and browns predominate. White markings on head and legs are permitted. Dark-eyed, pale palominos and very light chestnut are only allowed in mares and geldings.

TYPE A New Forest pony should be of the riding type with substance.

It should have a pony head, well set on, long sloping shoulders, strong quarters, plenty of bone, good depth of body, straight limbs and good hard round feet.

The larger ponies, although narrow enough for children, are

capable of carrying adults. The smaller ponies often show more quality. Judges are requested to give preference to ponies with depth and bone, even at the expense of quality.

ACTION Straight, with free movement, but not exaggerated with flicking toes. Over-refined heads are neither typical nor desirable.

Presentation

Youngstock are shown in a leather slip or in-hand bridle. Colts two years old and over are bitted.

If using a New Forest for other classes, such as BSPS classes, you will have to pull his mane and tail a little. Leave his mane long enough to look natural even though your plaits might be a bit big! His 'natural' looking tail can be coated in hair gel and then bandaged so that it looks like a pulled tail – even if it isn't.

THE SHETLAND PONY

THE SHETLAND PONY STUD BOOK is the oldest of the native stud books, being founded in 1890. The Shetland is also the smallest breed, and the strongest in relation to his size. One well-known story tells of a Shetland pony regularly carrying a 2.5cwt sack of meal twenty-six miles (42km) across country. A certain Mr Brand, on visiting the Shetland Islands in 1700, says that 'although the ponies are only nine or ten hands high, they are full of vigour and life and will carry a man and a woman behind him, 8 miles forward and as many back'.

His small size is thought to be due to the harsh conditions in the north of Scotland, although modern-day ponies bred all over England do not grow any bigger.

In 1847 an Act of Parliament forbade the use of children in mines, and the strong little Shetland pony was immediately in great demand as a pit pony. Only male horses were used, leaving the mares on the islands to breed, though unfortunately this reduced the quality of the stallions used on the islands and the Shetland Pony Stud Book Society was formed to improve the breed.

Although mainly used in the mines and on their native islands, the popularity of Shetlands increased with their use as children's ponies. Today, although numbers are bred by enthusiasts for showing in hand, it is as children's riding ponies that the Shetlands have really made their mark. The famous Shetland Grand National and the delightful scurry driving pairs

Shetland pony mare and foal owned by Mrs S. M. Gibson and shown by her daughter Julia. The mare is Lockinge Elspeth by Lockinge Giles out of Lockinge Enid; the foal is Coppice Eloise by Coppice Bandsman.

are just two areas in which this little pony makes his mark. Shetland ponies have even been the mascots of the Parachute Regiment since 1950. Many children learn to ride on a Shetland which has 'been in the family' for years.

Since 1955 a premium scheme for stallions has been operating in the islands, and a stallion inspection scheme was introduced throughout Britain in 1973. For the past ten years, a ridden performance scheme has been in operation, to encourage these versatile little ponies to compete against their larger cousins – in ridden and working hunter pony classes, amongst others. Every year, Shetlands qualify for the various championships in these classes. Sales are held every autumn in the islands, and at Aberdeen and Reading. A breed show, together with various other Shetland-only shows, are held each year.

The Shetland has in the past had a reputation for being 'difficult'. However, it is always important to remember that he is a very intelligent little pony and – he is a pony! He is not a pet dog or whatever and must be treated like any other 'horse'. If he is spoilt, he will use his intelligence to play games with you, just as any other pony which is spoilt. He is not a pony ever to be taken for granted.

Breed Standard

HEIGHT Registered stock must not exceed 40in at two years or under, nor 42in at four years or over. Ponies are measured from the withers to the ground by a measuring stick, and a level stance, preferably concrete, should be used.

COLOUR Shetland ponies may be any colour except spotted.

COAT The coat changes according to the seasons of the year; a double coat in winter, with guard hairs which shed the rain and keep the pony's skin completely dry in the worst of weather. By contrast, the summer coat is short and should carry a beautiful silky sheen. At all times, the mane and tail hair should be long, straight and profuse, and the feathering of the fetlocks straight and silky.

HEAD The head should be small, carried well, and in proportion. Ears should be small and erect, wide-set, but pointing well forward. Forehead should be broad with bold, dark, intelligent

Shetland pony Grand National, Surrey County Show, 1993.

eyes. Blue eyes are not acceptable. Muzzle must be broad with nostrils wide and open. Teeth and jaw must be correct.

FORELEGS Should be well placed, with sufficient good flat bone. Strong forearm. Short, balanced cannon bone. Springy pasterns.

HINDLEGS The thighs should be strong and muscular, with well shaped, strong hocks, neither hooky or too straight. When viewed from behind, the hindlegs should not be set too widely apart, nor should the hocks turn in.

FEET Tough, well shaped and round – not short, narrow, contracted or thin.

ACTION Straight, free action, using every joint and tracking up well.

GENERAL A most salient and essential feature of the Shetland pony is its general air and vitality (presence), its stamina and its robustness.

Presentation

The breed society allows ridden ponies to be clipped during the winter. The mane and tail should always be left full. Youngstock are shown in a leather bridle, with or without bit (two years or older), and a brass browband is permissible. It is often difficult to get a saddle to fit a ridden Shetland, and felt saddles are really not good enough for serious showing; cruppers are not desirable, either. We have found that the best saddle is a flat, fairly thin show saddle, held down by point straps at the front. A chamois leather used as a numnah also helps to stop slipping.

Welsh Ponies and Cobs

WELSH PONIES AND COBS are today divided into four sections: Section A, the Welsh Mountain pony; Section B, the Welsh pony; Section C, the pony of cob type; and Section D, the cob. The Section A is really the only section which can claim any great length of native history. It is said that Julius Caesar was supposed to have a stud of ponies in North Wales. It is also known, from parts of harness and bits which have been found dating back to Roman times, that the native animals at that time were around 12hh, the modern-day height limit for a Welsh Mountain pony.

Various Welsh ponies were registered in the original Polo Pony Stud Book or the Hackney Stud Book at the end of the last century, the Welsh Pony and Cob Society being founded in 1901. Previously ponies had only been divided into North Wales ponies and South Wales ponies, but with the publication of the first stud book by the new society, ponies were divided into four sections. At first they were designated Section A, Welsh Mountain ponies not exceeding 12.2hh; Section B, Welsh ponies of cob type between 12.2hh and 13.2hh; Section C, Welsh Cobs between 13.2hh and 14.2hh; and Section D, Welsh Cobs between 14.2hh and 15.2hh. By 1931 Section A ponies were only allowed to be up to 12hh, and at about the same time, Section B was altered to fulfil a need for children's riding ponies. So the cob-type ponies moved to Section C and the cobs became Section D only, with no upper height limit.

The Welsh breeds represent by far the largest proportion of native ponies in Britain today – in 1990 there were 34,720 stallions and 108,204 mares registered. Annual performance awards run by the Welsh Pony and Cob Society are supported by increasing numbers of ponies, and membership of the society is the largest of any native pony society in Britain today. The society presents its annual medals at affiliated shows. There are classes for all sections at the annual Royal Welsh Show, and recently the society has introduced a performance show; there is also an annual all-Welsh show at Northleach in Gloucestershire each summer. There are several sales at various locations throughout the year; and the *Welsh Pony and Cob Journal* is an annual publication which is read all over the world.

The Welsh Mountain Pony: Section A

Most of the mountain ponies bred today would have no chance of survival on the Welsh mountains, but thankfully their ancestors did survive the harsh climate – and they also survived the law of Henry VIII which prohibited the use of stallions under 15hh. The original mountain pony was usually a dark colour – bay, black or brown – with a much coarser coat than the present-day pony. Although in recent years there have been many well-known grey ponies, it is interesting to note that the first grey pony was not registered until 1894. It is possible that the grey colour came from Arab blood introduced to improve the native stock, and it is certainly easy to see the Arab influence in the dished face of the mountain ponies. One of the very best known of Section A sires was *Coed Coch Madog*, winning 139 first prizes and 63 championships, and many of today's champions have him in their pedigree.

Breed standard

GENERAL CHARACTER Hardy, spirited and pony-like.

COLOUR Any colour, except piebald and skewbald.

HEAD Small, clean cut, well set on and tapering to the muzzle.

The eyes should be bold and the ears well-placed, small and pointed; they should be well up on the head, and proportionately close. The nostrils should be prominent and open. Jaws and throat should be clean and finely cut, with ample room at the angle of the jaw.

NECK Lengthy, well-carried and moderately lean in the case of

Aston Tinkerbell, a Section A mare (1977) by Whatton Spritely out of Revel Chianti. Bred by Miss R. Russell-Allen, exhibited by the author, ridden by Anna Plotnek.

mares, but inclined to be cresty in the case of mature stallions.
SHOULDERS Long and sloping well back. Withers moderately fine, but not 'knifey'. The humerus upright so that the foreleg is not set in under the body.

FORELEGS Set square and true, not tied in at the elbows. Long, strong forearm; well-developed knee; short flat bone below knee, pasterns of proportionate slope and length, feet well shaped and round, hooves dense.

BODY Back and loins should be muscular, strong and well coupled. Girth should be deep, and the ribs well sprung.

HINDQUARTERS Lengthy and fine, not cobby, ragged or goose rumped. Tail set on well and carried gaily.

HIND LEGS Hocks to be large, flat and clean with points prominent, turning neither inwards nor outwards. The hind leg should not to be too bent. The hock set behind a line from the point of the quarter to the fetlock joint. Pasterns of proportionate slope and length. Feet well shaped, hooves dense.

ACTION Quick, free and straight from the shoulder, well away in front. Hocks well flexed with straight and powerful leverage, and well under the body.

The Welsh Pony, Section B

The original specification for this section would have more closely matched today's Section C pony: he would have been suitable for pulling a light cart, for shepherding and for other farm work. However, it became increasingly evident that there was a better market for children's riding ponies, particularly in England and so, the Welsh mares were crossed with Arab and Thoroughbred blood to produce a less stocky pony, more suitable for riding than driving. The well-known stallion *Tanybwlch Berwyn,* to whom so many of today's ponies trace back, was the result of a cross between a Welsh Mountain mare and a Barb stallion. In 1947 the section was closed to outside

Langshot Toytown, a Section B gelding (1983) by Gunthwaite Briar out of Hever Fenella. Bred by Miss A. Baldry, exhibited by the Forsyth family and ridden by Hugh Forsyth.

blood, and any pony crossed with Section C or D has to go into that section. Ponies crossed B with A can go into Section B.

The Section B pony of today is sometimes too light of bone and refined to be called a true native type. There has been too much movement towards the show pony – no doubt caused by market pressure. The breed standard says 'the general description of the ponies in Section A of the stud book is applicable to those in Section B, but more particularly the Section B shall be described as a riding pony, with quality, riding action, adequate bone and substance, hardiness and constitution and with pony character'. It is to be hoped that with the increase in popularity of the mountain and moorland classes we shall see more Section B ponies with 'adequate bone and substance'.

The Welsh pony of Cob Type: Section C

This is the original Section B of the stud book, and not – as is often thought today – the Section for Welsh Cobs which have not grown quite big enough! It is the pony of cob type; that is to say a pony with more bone and substance than a Section B, and taller in height than a Section A. They were often bred by crossing a cob with a mountain pony. By the 1950s this section had all but died out, and even today it remains the smallest section in numbers of ponies registered.

Numbers were increased again by using Section A blood – a good example is the well-known *Lyn Cwmcoed*, being sired by *Coed Coch Madog* (Section A) out of a cob-type mare.

Aston True Welshman, a Section C gelding by Glanllyn Ghia out of Hewid Bronwen. Bred by Miss R. Russell-Allen, exhibited by the author and ridden by Emma Williams.

The Welsh Cob: Section D

The origins of the Welsh Cob are lost in the mists of time, and there have been infusions in the past of many other bloods, including Arab, Thoroughbred, Norfolk Roadster and Hackney. However, from early Welsh literature it is known that the Welsh Cob was established as a breed in the fifteenth and the sixteenth centuries. These cobs were famed for their trotting ability. The stallions were often travelled around the principality serving mares, led by a boy or man on a pony.

Welsh Cobs have commanded huge prices at auction sales over the years and have been exported all over the world. Today they are in demand for crossing with the Thoroughbred to provide eventers, hunters and show jumpers, and as pure-breds for riding, driving and hunting.

Breed Standard – *Welsh Pony of Cob Type and Welsh Cob (Pony of cob type not to exceed 13.2hh)*

GENERAL CHARACTER Strong, hardy and active, with pony character and as much substance as possible.

COLOUR Any colour, except piebald and skewbald.

HEAD Must be full of quality and pony character – a coarse head and Roman nose are most objectionable. Eyes should be bold and prominent and set widely apart; ears neat and well set.

FRONT Neck should have good length and be well carried. Moderately lean in the case of mares, but inclined to be cresty in mature stallions. Shoulders should be strong, but well laid back.

FORELEGS Set square and not tied in at the elbows. Long, strong forearms. Knees well developed with abundance of bone below them. Pasterns of proportionate slope and length. Feet well shaped and hooves dense. When in the rough, a moderate quantity of silky feather is not objected to, but coarse wiry hair is definitely unacceptable.

MIDDLEPIECE Back and loins should be muscular and strong, and well coupled. Deep through heart and well ribbed up.

HINDQUARTERS Lengthy and strong. Ragged or drooping quarters are objectionable. Tail should be well set on.

HIND LEGS Second thighs, strong and muscular. Hocks should be large, flat and clean, with points prominent, turning neither inward or outward. The hind legs must not be too bent, and the hock should not be set behind a line falling from the point of the quarter to the fetlock joint. Pasterns of proportionate slope and length. Feet well shaped. Hooves dense.

ACTION Free, true and forcible. The knee should be bent and the whole foreleg should be extended straight from the shoulder and as far forward as possible in the trot. Hocks must flex under the body with straight and powerful leverage.

Tardebigge Esther, a Section D mare (1988) by Llanarth Solo out of Tardebigge Elsie. Bred and exhibited by Mr B. Abrey.

Other relevant rules

GELDINGS Welsh mountain pony geldings that have grown over 12hh and are over 5 years of age can be re-entered as Welsh pony geldings, thus enabling them to compete in Section B classes.

HEIGHT The following height limits for youngstock shall apply for animals registered in Sections B and C yearlings: 12.3hh; 2-year-olds, 13.0hh; 3-year-olds, 13.1hh.

BROOD MARES Three-year-old fillies are not eligible to compete in brood mare classes. Females are acknowledged as being mares when they are four years old and over.

WEIGHT OF SHOES For ponies not exceeding 13.2hh, no shoe shall exceed 1lb (0.4kg) in weight in the case of stallions, or 8oz (0.2kg) in the case of youngstock. For cobs and ponies exceeding 13.2hh and not exceeding 14hh, no shoe shall exceed 1.5lb (0.67kg). For animals exceeding 14hh, no shoe shall exceed 2lb (0.9kg), or in the case of yearling colts and fillies, 1.5lb (0.67kg).

Presentation

Although the rules of the society say 'animals registered in all sections should be shown in as natural a state as possible', most Welsh 'performers' are clipped in the winter. Section B ponies have their mane and tail pulled somewhat – although not to the extent of the show pony – and all sections can be trimmed carefully around the jaw. Feather should not be removed. If your Section A or B pony is needed to compete in classes under British Show Pony Society rules, where he will have his mane in plaits, you may need to shorten it slightly in order not to have plaits the size of golf balls. It is always difficult to achieve a compromise between the native state for mountain and moorland classes and the 'show pony' state of BSPS classes. And if you thought this book might give you an easy answer to that one, you will be sadly disappointed!

Welsh plait.

All Welsh sections can have a small section of mane behind the ear plaited, to separate the forelock from the mane. A thin blue or red ribbon can be plaited in to this plait. Tails are always left loose. Care should be taken not to flatten feather with bandages or boots.

Youngstock are shown either in a white halter or (usually for Section B ponies) a leather slip. Sections A and B ridden ponies should have a fairly fine bridle, which compliments their head. Sections C and D cobs should have a stouter bridle with a flat noseband. Cobs can be difficult to fit with a saddle: do make sure that your tree is wide enough.

The Societies

Pony Societies

The National Pony Society
Willingdon House
102 High Street
Alton
Hants GU34 1EN
Tel: 0420 88333

Ponies Association (UK) Ltd
Chesham House
56 Green End Road
Sawtry
Huntingdon
Cambs PE17 5UY
Tel: 0487 830278

Northern Counties Pony Association
Mrs L. Richardson
Corner Farm
Hinstock
Market Drayton
Shropshire TF9 2NG
Tel: 0952 550271

Breeds Societies

English Connemara Pony Society
2 The Leys
Salford
Chipping Norton
Oxon OX7 5FD

Dales Pony Society
196 Springvale Road
Walkley
Sheffield
South Yorkshire S6 3NU

Dartmoor Pony Society
Whitehorn Cottage
Hittisleigh
Exeter
Devon EX6 6LG

Exmoor Pony Society
Glen Fern
Waddicombe
Dulverton
Somerset TA22 9RY

The Fell Pony Society
Riccarton Mill
Newcastleton
Roxburghshire TD9 0SN

Highland Pony Society
Beechwood
Elie
Fife KY9 1DH

New Forest Pony and Cattle Breeding Society
Beacon Cottage
Burley
Ringwood
Hampshire BH24 4EW

Shetland Pony Stud Book Society
Pedigree House
Kings Place
Perth PH2 8AD

Welsh Pony and Cob Society
6 Chalybeate Street
Aberystwyth
Dyfed SY23 1HS

Index

Page numbers in *italics* refer to illustrations